Acclaim

Marva J. Dawn *author,* Being Well When We're Ill
Using profound and stimulating stories, Arnold welcomes us into an
elegant fabric of elderly life, abundant with significance. I know you
will find this book spiritually enriching.

Sr. Carol Keehan *president, Catholic Health Association*
This book gently invites us to reflect on the gift of aging more than
the challenge of aging, and reminds us in a wonderfully consoling
way that we age in the care of our gracious God.

Dr. Megan Best *bioethicist and palliative care practitioner*
How refreshing to read a book that describes the enrichment that
comes with the passing of time. With the author we can celebrate
the joys of imperfection; the importance of a sense of humor as we
age; and the importance of giving thanks for what our years have
given us. This is timely wisdom.

Tim Costello *chief executive, World Vision Australia*
Arnold is a trusted fellow traveler and guide. His book encouraged
me to reflect on my own journey, and I am excited about my future.
I hope that it will have the same impact on you.

Fleming Rutledge *author,* The Undoing of Death
What a wonderful book! For those who care about their elders, it
provides a treasury of wisdom. For those of us facing the years of
declining powers, this is a gold mine of encouragement. I will refer
to this book often and recommend it to others.

Cardinal Cassidy *president emeritus, PCPCU, the Vatican*
I have found much in these pages for reflection and comfort and
hope this book will reach many who are in need of such consolation
and understanding as the years mount up.

Richard J. Foster *author,* Celebration of Discipline
Rich in Years is rich in wisdom, rich in courage, rich in hope. The people we meet in these pages and the stories they tell all build in us a confident assurance that God is with us every step of our journey.

Ian Harper *professor emeritus, University of Melbourne*
The key to finishing our days well, writes Arnold, is to cultivate thankfulness for each new day and to devote our time to the love and service of others. Wise words indeed, and especially comforting for those whose days are numbered – and isn't that all of us?

Catherine Wiley *founder, Catholic Grandparents Association*
An inspirational read for grandparents and indeed people of all ages. It deals sensitively with so many issues relating to aging and infirmity that people do not like to talk about, but really should. I found *Rich in Years* beautiful, helpful, and full of love.

Stephen Judd *chief executive, HammondCare*
Arnold does us all a great service by encouraging us to see aging as a part of the normal progress of life. Its challenges are to be faced with hope and in community rather than alone and in despair. This book is full of wisdom, encouragement, sadness and joy.

Hashim Garrett *speaker, Breaking the Cycle*
Reading this book is rewarding but hazardous – you will need to invest in a box of tissues as well. The introduction alone made me reach for them. Powerful.

Steve Auty *chief executive, Pilgrims Hospices*
Rich in Years does not shy away from the difficult aspects of aging – loss of faculties, health issues, loneliness, and facing the end of life. But its wise insights, often told through touching real-life stories, ring true and point the way to a more hopeful and humane path for older people and their families and caregivers.

Rich in Years

Rich in Years

*Finding Peace and Purpose
in a Long Life*

Johann Christoph Arnold

The Plough Publishing House

Published by The Plough Publishing House
Walden, New York
Robertsbridge, England
Elsmore, Australia
www.plough.com

Cover photo: © Corbis Images
Scripture taken from the Holy Bible, New International Version. © 1973, 1978, 1984, 2011 by Biblica, Inc.
Used by permission. All rights reserved worldwide.

ISBN: 978-0-87486-897-5

FIRST U.S. PRINTING AUG. 2013: 60,000	FIRST U.K. PRINTING AUG. 2013: 15,000
SECOND U.S. PRINTING SEP. 2013: 30,000	SECOND U.K. PRINTING AUG. 2013: 5,000
FIRST AU PRINTING AUG. 2013: 5,000	THIRD U.K. PRINTING SEP. 2013: 15,000

A catalog record for this book is available from the British Library.

Library of Congress Cataloging-in-Publication Data

Arnold, Johann Christoph, 1940-
Rich in years : finding peace and purpose in a long life / Johann Christoph
Arnold.
    pages cm
ISBN 978-0-87486-897-5 (pbk.)
1. Older Christians--Religious life. 2. Aging--Religious aspects--Christi-
anity. I. Title.
BV4580.A76 2013
248.8'5--dc23
                        2013028113

Printed in the USA

My wife, Verena, and I dedicate this book
to our parents, Heinrich and Annemarie Arnold
and Hans and Margrit Meier. Because both these couples
remained faithful in marriage and faithful to Jesus,
their lives were richly fulfilled into old age,
and touched thousands of others.

Contents

Foreword

by Cardinal Seán O'Malley

I N T H I S B O O K, Johann Christoph Arnold has once again offered us a translation of the meaning of God's love for us through all the days of our lives. Here he shares with us a meditation on what Teilhard de Chardin called "passive diminishment" – the human experience of aging and suffering.

What's remarkable in these pages is how Arnold unifies so many of the strands that run through his previous books. For example, he expands on his book on marriage and human sexuality – *Sex, God and Marriage* – by describing the love of husband and wife that is both within history and yet simultaneously related to God's eternal love.

Similarly, he builds on his book *Why Forgive?*, which focuses on the centrality of forgiveness and mercy as the basis of peace, reminding us of the mercy that we each receive. He calls us to allow that mercy to work in us by forgiving others, and so enter into the life of eternity.

Crucially, Arnold also highlights the importance of prayer: "Whatever time on earth we have, we should use it to lead others to a deeper, more prayerful relationship with God. This is perhaps the greatest gift we can give."

Arnold's work thus reflects the heart of Pope Francis's first encyclical, *Lumen Fidei* ("The Light of Faith"). Here Pope Francis adopts the work of Pope Benedict XVI while adding his own insights to his predecessor's important engagement with Scripture and tradition, stating:

> There is an urgent need to see once again that faith is a light. For once the flame of faith dies out, all other lights begin to dim. The light of faith is unique, since it is capable of illuminating every aspect of human existence. A light this powerful cannot come from ourselves but from a more primordial source: in a word it must come from God...Faith, received from

God as a supernatural gift, becomes a light for our way, guiding our journey through time.

In keeping with this vision, the Roman Catholic Church is now embarking on the "new evangelization" – a process of renewal through the Holy Spirit's gifts, leading to an invigoration of our witness to the gospel. As Pope Benedict has reminded us, this renewal is closely linked to the call to unity among all Jesus' followers, across denominational boundaries:

> The spiritual poverty of many of our contemporaries, who no longer perceive the absence of God from their life as a deprivation, constitutes a challenge to all Christians. In this context, we believers in Christ are asked to return to the essential, to the heart of our faith, to bear witness together to the world to the living God, that is, to a God who knows and loves us, under whose gaze we live; of a God who expects the response of our love in everyday life. (Address to the Pontifical Council for Promoting Christian Unity, November 15, 2012)

It is a joy to be able to acknowledge in Johann Christoph Arnold's book a manifestation of what

Pope Francis and Pope Benedict describe. The work of Pastor Arnold and the community to which he belongs, the Bruderhof, is a testimony to the bond of faith that we as Christians share.

Cardinal Seán Patrick O'Malley, O.F.M. Cap.
Archbishop of Boston

Preface

by Rolland G. Smith

Years ago I did a television interview with Ruth
Gordon, the actress, and her husband Garson Kanin.
They were in their mid-seventies at the time. I asked
them, "What is the hardest thing for you two as you
move into your senior years?" In unison they said,
"Losing your friends." And then Ruth said to me, "I
would encourage all old people to make friends of
various generations – ten years younger, twenty, thirty,
forty. Make friends; be a friend."

I think that is wonderful advice. As I age (I am
now in my seventies, like Johann Christoph Arnold),
I find that I have some difficulty relating to my
teenage grandchildren. So I always look for the
connection between what was and what is now. I find
it interesting when my grandkids call me up and say,

"You experienced such and such. What was it like? We are studying that in history class." All children love stories, so this sharing is extremely important to create a commonality between the younger generation and the older.

One of the low points of our Western culture was when we decided that a three-car garage was more important than a room for an aging aunt or uncle or grandparent. The proliferation of nursing homes is something I detest; most old people should be living with the family and dying at home. We live in the "me generation." Hopefully there is a way to get away from the "me generation" to the "we generation." How can we create connections between generations when the young and the old no longer even live in the same places?

I've spent a lot of time in native cultures, watching how they integrate with one another. One of the most profound experiences was with the Embera Indians, an indigenous tribe of Panama. I took a boat up the Chagres River and spent some time with them at their camp. They prepared a wonderful meal of tilapia that they had just caught on the river and cooked it on an open fire. But they also did a dance. And when they dance, the younger and the older dance together as a community, the younger holding on to the older, and the older holding on to the younger. What a powerful image: each group appreciates and needs the other. I think we can learn from this. While some of us might feel *less* useful to society after we retire or slow down, maybe we can learn from other cultures that our place in the dance of life is actually getting *more* important.

In this book, Johann Christoph Arnold answers a lot of the questions that my wife Ann and I ponder as we get older. We certainly deal with small difficulties that crop up every day. We've always done certain things; I'll take out the garbage and she'll vacuum. But we have found as we get older, it's important not to expect that to continue to happen. What's important is to say "thank you" and to appreciate the gift of living together.

Illness is another big factor in aging. (Ann and I know what that's like; she's had four cancers.) If you are infirm you've got to be willing to change. You can't stay stuck in what used to be. But it's not only in big things like cancer. Small changes are necessary too. I find as I get older, I can't lift things the way I used to; I have to ask for help.

As I age, it takes more effort to be tolerant of some of the junk that I see in the world. Perhaps "tolerance" is not the right word; I don't agree with much of what I see in government and in popular culture. Still, I try to be enthusiastic about new things, because that helps keep you young and in touch with the younger generation. The word "enthusiasm" is really interesting. Its root word is *theos* (God), so it basically means, "inspired by God."

Ann and I also think about dying and about life after death. I really don't fear death. If we believe what we say we believe, we should be ready to go any time. If we've finished what we came here to do, why would we want to stay in this time and density when what is next is so glorious and wonderful?

I also have no doubt that there is a heaven. Maybe that comes with age, or maybe it's a gift from God that allows you to understand things if you take the time to think about them. Take the time to see the absolute joy of living in this time and place, to appreciate a summer rain, or flowers in a garden. Longfellow writes:

> For age is opportunity no less
> Than youth itself, though in another dress,
> And as the evening twilight fades away
> The sky is filled with stars, invisible by day.

In this book, Johann Christoph Arnold helps us to see these stars. I thank him for taking the time to write it.

Rolland G. Smith, former CBS news anchor

Introduction

by the author

M<small>Y WIFE AND I LOVE TO HIKE</small>, and over the years we have met countless people on the trail. Some are young and vigorous, with new equipment and a spring in their step. They may act like they know what they are doing, but in many ways they are naïve and inexperienced. Others move with a steadiness and confidence that come from having passed over this ground before. And some, quite frankly, are lost. They don't know where they are coming from or where they are going.

This is our human experience. In *The Pilgrim's Progress,* John Bunyan compares life to a long journey. Bunyan's pilgrim knows his ultimate goal, but he constantly battles dangers along the way: tempting distractions, ferocious beasts, and trackless swamps.

Often the way is narrow, edged with steep cliffs and a plummeting abyss. As the pilgrim nears the finish, he is attacked more than ever. So too is life. In old age, we begin to lose our faculties in ways younger folks can't imagine, and sickness, loneliness, and death itself loom ever larger.

Every journey is plagued with doubts about whether we'll reach our final destination. Often, we get hurt along the way. Broken and disoriented, we struggle on. This is always harder if we walk alone. The surest way to stay safely on the path is to help one another. Whether a veteran traveler or novice, we are all on this journey together. Striking out alone, as any weathered outdoorsman will tell you, is the quickest way to lose your bearings.

When we experience hardship, we gain knowledge of the trail that can and should be shared with others. We know the most stunning views and the importance of stopping to appreciate them. We know the secret springs that never run dry, and where to safely stop and rest. In the same way, we who have reached old age can be a source of wisdom, hope, and inspiration for others. That is why I wrote this book. I have stumbled frequently and lost the way more times than I care to admit. But I do know what might make the journey less fearful and more fulfilling. I hope the stories in this book will encourage you to keep on going. And so I dedicate this book to my fellow seniors, wishing them strength to continue helping other pilgrims.

All seasoned hikers carry a compass. They may not use it for many days, but when they do, it will quickly direct their steps again. On my own journey, the most important guide for staying on track has been prayer. When I turn to God, and away from my worries about the road ahead, he points my heart anew to the final goal. Peace of heart also comes from a daily focus on forgiveness and from service to others. These are tools we can use as we travel on.

In the end, it is God, not we, who determines the length of time we spend on the trail. Each of our journeys begins at birth and ends at death. Some of us walk for years, losing the trail occasionally, only to come across it again. Or we backtrack to help a straggler along the way, perhaps wondering if we're not wasting our precious time. Others travel only a short time, but even so, who can say that they, too, have not reached the goal set for them by God?

But each of us does reach the end, and there Jesus will be watching and waiting for us to arrive. He knows when we started out, and he has watched our every step. He will judge us if we have passed by or ignored a struggling traveler without reaching out a helping hand. But he will reward us for every deed of love that we may have done for others, and he will welcome us with open arms: "Come to me, all you who are weary and burdened, and I will give you rest" (Matt. 11:28).

Rudi Hildel
"I may be growing older, but don't fuss over me!"

1

Growing Older

Grow old along with me!
The best is yet to be,
The last of life, for which the first was made:
Our times are in His hand
Who saith "A whole I planned,
Youth shows but half; trust God:
    see all, nor be afraid!"

Robert Browning

THIS POEM IS A FAVORITE of Ellen Keiderling's, a former secretary of mine who was a great help on many of my other books. Although she no longer works for me, she is a vibrant member of my church and often contributes when there is an opportunity for open discussion. When I first got inspired to write this book, Ellen wrote the following:

Although I am eighty, and struggling with old age, I don't want to go back to twenty-five. These are the best years of my life.

In my old age, I know that it is important that someone helps me. As Jesus told Peter, "When you were younger you dressed yourself and went where you wanted; but when you are old you will stretch out your hands, and someone else will dress you and lead you where you do not want to go" (John 21:18). I am certainly being led where I don't want to go, and this is hard to accept.

I don't always like it when people boss me around and hover over me. I don't really need help with getting dressed – but I do appreciate it. I don't like it when people walk with me everywhere – but I appreciate it because I am getting older. And I am so glad to be at peace. What Browning writes is so true – I have no reason to be afraid.

Not all of us are like Ellen. The fear of death coupled with the fear of growing older fills our minds, but we don't want to talk about it. What is it that we are trying to avoid? I wonder if it isn't these simple truths from Shakespeare, who wrote (I still know these lines from having to memorize them in high school):

All the world's a stage,
And all the men and women merely players:
They have their exits and their entrances...

(As You Like It)

Out, out, brief candle!
Life's but a walking shadow, a poor player
That struts and frets his hour upon the stage,
And then is heard no more; it is a tale
Told by an idiot, full of sound and fury,
Signifying nothing.

(Macbeth)

Many of us worry that no matter how successful our lives have been, they will fade into oblivion and soon be forgotten. Or we may fear losing our mind, our memory, and our independence. We also fear loneliness, pain, and suffering. Many worry that they have not lived as they should. But all this can be overcome. Growing old doesn't have to be a prison of hopelessness and despair. It can present us with unique opportunities, where life's meaning and purpose find fulfillment and where we can express the love we've always wanted to but somehow were never able.

Our society has lost perspective on growing old. Advances in medicine have given us a false sense of immortality. We seem to think we can live forever and pride ourselves on pushing the limits of age, but by doing so we push God out of our lives. In idolizing youth, vigor, and bodily health, we become obsessed with increasing life's length, but God is concerned with deepening life's meaning.

There is an entire industry dedicated to helping us rebel against the physical symptoms of growing old. The myriad cosmetics, pharmaceuticals, and exercise programs tailored to the elderly all try to convince us that being young is the only way to be. But realistically, by the time we are in our seventies, each of us has at least begun to lose some of our abilities. Our hair gets grayer (if it's there at all), our skin more wrinkled, and our gait slower. Why can't we accept this?

God certainly accepts us as we grow old. Scripture makes it quite clear that God loves the aged and holds them in high regard. Shouldn't we do the same? A long life is a blessing from God, and with it comes a responsibility to the next generation.

There are many stories of God using old people to accomplish his purposes. Abraham and Sarah were already old when their son Isaac was born. Moses was eighty years old when he led God's people out of Egypt. Zechariah and Elizabeth were "well along in years" when John the Baptist was born to them. If we could have even an inkling of the ways of God, we would find that growing old does not have to be a slow decline. We do not need to assume that our best days are behind us.

Those who retain a sense of adventure as their health declines will be able to face the indignities of old age with grace and good humor. John Hinde, who gave up a budding business career at Lloyd's of London to join a rural farming community, was one of my role models during childhood. A lifetime later he told me:

> When I was twenty-one, life was a great adventure. Now everything is somehow so sedate. Of course at eighty-three, I don't have quite the same urge for adventure as I did at twenty-one. But when you think of it, growing old is an adventure! It's something you've got to go at with daring. You lose one thing

after another and become more dependent and more stupid and all kinds of things, but still it should be an adventure.

Of course, not everyone has such a positive outlook on growing old. Embracing the aging process and the approaching end of our life is never easy.

Rudi Hildel, a close friend since childhood, was a widower in his eighties. He wanted to stay independent, even though it was obvious that he needed more assistance with daily activities. We had many fiery discussions about how he felt fussed over, when he simply wished to be left alone. He once told me:

> Yes, I am getting older and people are lovingly concerned with my health, but it can go too far. This "over-concern" is a big problem for me. I'm constantly asked, "Can you really go alone?" "Shall I lend you my arm?" "Be careful, you may catch a cold!" "Careful – you may fall and break a hip!"

Rudi's stubborn streak would almost cause his downfall. He had an electric scooter, and as it became clear that he could no longer drive it safely, his son-in-law took away the keys. But Rudi cajoled one of his grandsons into finding them, and soon he was driving again. Next, the family called on an electrician to more permanently disable the scooter, but again, Rudi convinced a grandson to do some clandestine repair work, and he was on the road again. A few days later, driving down a steep gravel path, he lost control of the scooter and began going through a ditch and down an embankment. Only the chance presence of a passerby, who grabbed the back of the seat and hung on tight, prevented a catastrophe.

It was only then that Rudi realized the danger of his independent streak. The scooter was put in storage, and though reluctant at first, he learned to accept being pushed in a wheelchair.

Eileen Robertshaw, a feisty Englishwoman, was in excellent health well into old age. She swam regularly until she reached her eighties. But eventually, she found a silver lining in the act of relying on others.

There seem to be two temptations as we grow older. One is to take advantage of any help that might be offered to us and become lazy and self-indulgent. The other is to be too intent on independence. Yielding to the first makes one spineless and selfish; yielding to the other can absorb our strength and attention at the expense of our relationships with other people.

The latter (at least in me) is due to vanity. I was proud that I could do something that others my own age or younger couldn't do as easily. Like all vanity, it is absurd. It is no merit of mine if I retain some faculty or the other, and in any case, it is unkind because I am putting myself above others.

When I finally decided to get a caregiver, life became enriched in ways I had not imagined. In becoming more dependent, I had more time and opportunity for interaction with others. Even if I didn't need a proffered arm, I learned to say, "I don't really need it, but I'd love to have your company." My philosophy is, keep going as much and as long as you can, but don't let it isolate you.

Growing older, as Rudi and Eileen discovered, certainly does involve a battle, because so much of what we have known is coming to an end. The Welsh poet Dylan Thomas captured this in his famous poem, "Do not go gentle into that good night," writing:

Old age should burn and rave at close of day;
Rage, rage against the dying of the light.

One could argue that most of us are actually trying to find peace in old age rather than rage, and in my view the light never really dies. However, giving everything we have to our last breath is certainly something we should aspire to. This is a paradox: death is the final enemy, and we must fight it to the end with all life's vigor, yet we know that Christ has conquered death, so we need not fear it.

Growing older can be a gift, but only if we surrender ourselves to God's plan. Then we can stop complaining about things we can't do anymore and realize that God is finding new ways to use us. With this gift from God we can encourage many others. When we find the peace of Jesus, it will more than replace the things we used to do for personal satisfaction. Even with our physical and mental abilities curtailed, we have many opportunities to work for humanity and for God's kingdom on earth by living out the two main commandments of Jesus: "Love the Lord your God with all your heart and with all your soul and with all your mind," and "Love your neighbor as yourself" (Matt. 22:37–39).

Josua Dreher
"Why are we afraid of eternity?"

2

Accepting Changes

OLD AGE CREEPS UP on everyone. Most of my life I didn't want to think about it. Then obstacles began to appear, trying to slow me down. First I lost my voice and could not speak for months. Then I had trouble with my heart. Both of my eyes needed surgery, and one eye is completely blind. Then my hearing deteriorated. It seemed like one thing after another was breaking down.

Thankfully my wife and I still walk a few miles every day. I can still read and type enough to do my work. Still, how many of us are like the friend of mine who once exclaimed, "My body is aging, but I am not!" I'm sure many find themselves in similar states of denial. Naturally, letting go of all the activities that we used to do is difficult. It can be hard to accept our changing role in the family or workplace as others take over our responsibilities. This can make us feel useless and depressed.

A sense of humor about the trials of old age is more important than we realize. Laughter can brighten the days of all those around us who think they are too busy with important things to joke around. Sometimes laughter is the only answer when we forget people's names or where we put our keys. My doctor, who is older than me, once joked, "All my friends walk faster than they used to. They also talk faster and quieter. They even look a little fuzzier. Everything's changing! Or is it me?" As my friend Pete Seeger likes to sing:

> Old age is golden, or so I've heard said,
> But sometimes I wonder, as I crawl into bed,
> With my ears in a drawer, my teeth in a cup,
> My eyes on the table until I wake up...

Less of a laughing matter is a loss of mobility, starting with the need for canes and progressing to walkers, wheelchairs, and bed rest. All these things encroach on our independence, and we find that activities that were once easy now require effort and stamina. No wonder the bumper sticker says, "Old age is not for sissies!"

Other aspects of growing old are even more difficult to bear: the death of a spouse or the onset of dementia. Sudden illness strikes and one is confronted with one's own mortality. These are very real fears, and ones I've dealt with personally.

Often, too, we have regrets about the past. We may feel we didn't succeed in our chosen career, earn as much as we could have, or advance as far as we deserved. We may wish we had raised our children differently. Personally, I feel I have missed far too many opportunities to show love to other people.

But dwelling on these thoughts only creates bitterness and isolates us from others, even from beloved family members. The best way to deal with the mess we may have made of our lives, or the difficult burdens we may carry, is to accept God's grace as we face the future.

Perhaps this is the key to making the most of one's last years. Instead of focusing on our regrets, we can choose to give thanks to God for the life we have lived. Meister Eckhart said that with the advancing of age there should eventually be only one phrase left in our vocabulary – "Thank you." Such a feeling of gratitude doesn't come easily. But when it does, we realize that an exciting phase of our lives is starting in which we can still contribute, in new ways, to the good of humankind.

Leslie Underwood, a single sixty-five-year-old woman in my church, has been blind since her youth. Rather than rebelling against the added difficulties of aging, she discovered a better way.

Old age is a blessing to me. God's grace and wisdom have led me to a more peaceful life. And I'm realizing that old age can be a gift given to the young. Did you ever notice how very young children are attracted to the elderly? Isn't that part of God's plan?

When I die, I hope it will be seen as a gift to those who are so fearful and perplexed about the end of their own lives. I used to think of death as a dark and mysterious valley of transition to be avoided. But since becoming a Christian about fifteen years ago, eternity became real, and much of my fear of death has gone. I wait for the Lord's promises and can truthfully ask, "Death, where is thy sting?"

I do still have regrets about the past. Mine was not an easy life; I was raised in a chaotic environment with alcohol, violence, parental absences, and neglect. But I was able to move beyond myself by becoming a social worker and helping people whom others didn't want. For some of them, their fear of death was more real and immediate than mine. Now I live with other Christians, and the fear and distrust is slowly melting away, replaced by acceptance and love, which leads to spiritual peace.

I often wonder how to help an older person accept and embrace God's will. It is so important to help others rather than think only of ourselves. If we miss these opportunities, turning in on ourselves and losing sight of others, we easily lose perspective and become bitter or angry. Most of all, we need to learn how to forgive the hurts done by others. When we forgive, we become free and begin to see countless opportunities to contribute.

Retiring from one's job can provide time to make these contributions. Unfortunately, many approach retirement either as a time to fulfill their dreams, for their own pleasure, or as a time to dread, with empty, lonely hours. It is without a doubt a drastic change; for instance, learning to get along with one's spouse again after years of being out of the house for much of the day. We may miss the responsibilities and authority we had at work. Or we may simply miss being busy. But if we find something to live for, a cause or purpose that needs dedication and work, then we'll always have a reason to get up in the morning! In the last years, I have found fulfillment in speaking to high school and college students about forgiveness and reconciliation as part of a program called Breaking the Cycle.

One need not be physically fit to serve. Well into his eighties, Peter Cavanna, who was fluent in several languages, would go once a week to visit prisoners in the local jail. When the inmates moved to other prisons, he would keep in touch with them by mail. Eventually he corresponded with nearly forty men, in both Spanish and English. Peter's correspondence with inmates not only encouraged them, which they often expressed, but also fulfilled him in his last years. He would often tell those around him how his pen pals were doing.

Everyone can find some sort of fulfillment. It is so important to give thanks each day for some small thing of beauty, whether a sunrise, a birdsong, or a child's smile. There might be a plant on the windowsill or a bird feeder on the back porch that needs tending. Never miss the chance to offer a smile or a kind word to someone else, a friend or a stranger, or your spouse. If we are still able to read – now that we finally have time! – we may catch up on the classics of literature. Or just listen to great classical music. I have always loved the works of composers like Bach and Handel.

I've always enjoyed a good meal and a cold beer with my family and friends on the weekend. What could be more wonderful than breaking bread with others? As Jesus said, "For where two or three gather in my name, there am I with them" (Matt. 18:20). Anything that leads to community adds richness to our lives.

Of course, building community takes time. But that's another thing I've learned in my old age: to stop rushing around from one appointment to the next, and instead, to take more time with my wife, my children, my grandchildren, and other children in the neighborhood. Time spent alone is also valuable. Contemplative silence outdoors appreciating God's creation is beneficial to soul and body. Sometimes just "being" is more important than "doing."

Josua Dreher, one of my wife's cousins, is an excellent example of someone who, despite many odds, found fulfillment in such simple "being" at the end of his life. We grew up together in Paraguay. Life in the jungle was exciting, but also difficult. When Josua was a teenager his mother died unexpectedly and left nine children behind. This affected him deeply.

A few years later Josua moved to America. He befriended a young woman and became engaged to be married. Then, days before the wedding, he broke off the engagement and returned to Paraguay, without so much as a "goodbye" to his fiancée and friends.

We later found out he had become a cowboy, living in the back country. He settled down, married a Paraguayan woman, and raised a family. Then more tragedy struck. His first son died in infancy. He soldiered on, until his second son died from cancer at age twenty-two. Within a year, his wife died of a broken heart.

Josua knew that his life was not what it should be. He began seeking some resolution, some peace of heart, and after nearly forty years he returned to America. He very quickly made peace with everyone he had hurt when he left so abruptly many years before.

Remarkably, Josua did not dwell on his past failures or on the terrible misfortunes he had suffered. Rather, he continually expressed his gratitude for everything life had given him. He started giving arts and crafts lessons in an after-school program to pass on his knowledge of carpentry and leatherworking. Josua loved the children and taught them to appreciate the wonders and beauties of nature and to respect God's creation.

A short while later he was diagnosed with cancer himself. But a hard life in rugged lands had toughened him, and he suffered without complaint. He lived completely in the present, neither dwelling on the past nor fearing the future. Children flocked to visit him, surrounding his bed with crayoned pictures and scraggly bouquets. As the end of his life approached, thankfulness, rather than bitterness, radiated from his face. He was a man at peace with his Maker.

We all must find ways to play the hand life has dealt us. Physical pain and broken relationships can be redeemed by turning to other people. Alice von Hildebrand, a former philosophy professor in New York, is now in her nineties. She has found old age easier to accept because she has a reason for living.

When I was still teaching, I rode on the subway and looked at the faces: boredom, despair, sadness. This, in the richest country in the world!

But the moment that you relate to God – and thank him for your existence, for loving you, for being your savior – you can establish a most beautiful relationship with other people. You love and help one another. You realize the meaning of your life is not luxury and fun, but it is helping. Once you radiate joy, sooner or later people are going to say, "What's her secret?" And then gently, without preaching, without saying "I'm superior to you," you just share. After all, the meaning of the word "gospel" is "the happy message."

That's all we can do. Obviously there are moments of darkness and discouragement. There are moments when we lose sight of the beauty of the sky because there are clouds. But one very fine day you come out of it. We are made for joy. Don't expect Paradise on this earth. But there is meaning, and this meaning is the love of God.

All of us can find such meaning in our lives. When we do, we will also find strength and grace to accept the changes that come with age.

Alice von Hildebrand
"We are made for joy."

3

Combatting Loneliness

Even those of us who on the surface have the old age of their dreams will admit that feelings of emptiness and loneliness affect us all. How many elderly people dine alone each evening, or live alone in assisted-living centers, financially supported by their children miles away? Some of you may be reading this book in a nursing home or shut in your own apartment.

In each of us, there is a longing to live in community, to share whatever we have with others. God created us as communal beings, not as hermits. It does not matter whether we are old or young, sick or healthy. We belong together, and this togetherness brings fulfillment. We innately know this, of course. Many veterans tell me they returned for multiple tours of duty overseas because of the sense of family and community they felt with their fellow soldiers. Former gang members have also told me that their "street family" was closer and stronger than their biological family. In schools, coaches and teachers often find they are the only ones providing a family for their students.

As society becomes more fragmented, it is often the old who suffer most. They hurt for a sense of family and community. In my experience, we need to live in communal settings, where we can not only be looked after, but also continue to contribute and love and share. In Galatians we are told to "carry each other's burdens, and in this way fulfill the law of Christ" (Gal. 6:2). This means feeding the hungry, clothing the naked, and caring for the sick.

Ken Johnson, a retired physician, worked overseas for many years. After returning to the United States, he eventually founded several organizations that addressed the issues of caring for the elderly.

Old age should not be a withdrawal from the mainstream of society, yet older people themselves contribute to the social stereotype of their uselessness. Instead of looking forward to a more pleasant but still meaningful life, or making a difference in the lives of others, many accelerate the aging process by hanging out only with other seniors, sitting for hours in front of the TV, eating snacks, scanning only the headlines of the tabloids, and taking multiple pills from the many doctors they regularly visit. From this, many become depressed or succumb to alcoholism.

In every community there are very old people who live alone with serious disability and without adequate family, social, and financial supports. Their children and grandchildren are dispersed to far distances or live in spaces insufficient for accommodating an aged parent. But growing old with dignity is very much dependent on the three generation family or its equivalent of neighbors and community who surrogate for the extended family.

To combat these problems, I envisioned a multitude of the nation's churches, temples, and mosques forming local interfaith coalitions to recruit and train volunteers, many of them elderly themselves, to serve the needs of people with serious disability and with inadequate social support, and in so doing fulfill their spiritual destiny. The world's great religions all call upon their adherents to give succor to the helpless.

In our programs, volunteers handled a person's mail, saw that checks went to the bank, that utility bills were paid, and that there was enough food in the refrigerator. The volunteers came alive with a simple task like driving an elderly person to a doctor's office, doing minor repairs to steps and banisters, or changing a light bulb.

The elderly care receivers experienced a reprieve from their sense of abandonment and worthlessness. Their sense of dignity was restored. They could get a hot bath. Their hair and clothes were in good order. They were somebody because somebody showed concern for their well-being. Those who had mistrust about "government" social workers trusted and looked forward to "folks from the church."

One caregiver wrote me once that before he became a volunteer he spent his day keeping busy doing things like visiting with his grandchildren. He was content to do so, but since becoming a volunteer, he said, he felt "special" because now "someone *really* depends on me."

The benefits of these programs were enormous, even if nothing "big" was done. Everything was a small yet important service of love to another human being.

People of all professions can serve gallantly for years, and be famous, important, and have many friends, yet in old age they too quickly are forgotten. God has a different measure of human worth. As we grow older, we should reconsider how we value one another's contributions. We don't have to stand out or wave our special accomplishments in front of others.

Charlie Simmons found new happiness in his advanced age, in little ways. His contributions to society were not great, but they were important. A life-long New Yorker, he moved upstate after a career driving trucks and buses. After his beloved wife, Margie, died, he started to join us for dinner and worship services.

It didn't take much time for Charlie to feel completely at home. He missed no chance to point people to the peace and happiness he'd found in his simple and childlike faith, and he noticed when someone else was having a bad day. He would often claim that he kept a low profile, but would say it with a laugh, since he knew that it couldn't be further from the truth: standing over six feet tall, he preferred to shout everything from the rooftops, and he could not stand it when people whispered. He liked to loudly tell people, "You sing well," or "You're looking good for your age," or "I think you've lost weight!"

He loved to tell a good story, like about the time he ate thirty-four pancakes in a competition and had to "unload" them behind a tree on the way home (which he claimed is growing incredibly well as a result), or about the time he fell asleep during collection at church and they took his check out of his pocket anyway. But he was at his best when he was reaching out to others, bringing flowers – or ice cream or local apples – for a birthday or anniversary.

Charlie had a deep love for Jesus. After he started attending our church, I spoke many times with him about adult baptism and the forgiveness of sins. He was also never afraid to witness to Jesus. In our church services he always responded with a strong "Amen" when someone was preaching. And whenever we'd sing a hymn, invariably a loud "Praise God!" would follow the last stanza.

Charlie showed me how simple it can be to combat loneliness and depression. The possibilities are endless.

Is there a child near you that needs one-on-one time with an adult? Invite him over to play a game, help him with school work, or read him a story. An elderly neighbor may need someone to accompany her to an appointment – or she may just need remembering with a card on her birthday. It is only when we dwell on our past, using our old measure of self-worth, that our bodies seem decrepit in comparison. If we look at what we can give, rather than our limitations, we will be able to accept our new role.

Part of what might make us hesitate to rely more on other people is that we think we are a burden to them. This was not a problem for Charlie with his outgoing and boisterous personality. But we don't all have that confidence. Perhaps you've been made to feel that you are a burden by your own family, or perhaps you've been pushed out of a company or organization before you felt your usefulness was spent. I know people who are dearly loved and cared for, but still feel like a burden, because everything has to be done for them. Such feelings of guilt are real, but they are not insurmountable if we can find a humility that accepts and embraces our new station.

Charles Sinay discovered this when illness took his abilities away, and he had to find, after a lifetime of teaching and helping others, how to accept help himself. To receive this help, he had to physically be with other people, in community. At first this was hard, but eventually his feelings of uselessness and depression turned to joy.

Charles loved languages, and after receiving several advanced degrees, he spent years teaching English in places like Korea, Japan, the Pacific Islands, and Central America. Though an accomplished linguist, Charles's greatest love was reserved for the countless children he taught over the years. In fact, it was teaching that compromised his own health and significantly shortened his life: after years of resting his elbow on the edge of children's desks while giving individual assistance, he developed a bursitis that became seriously infected – and landed him in the ICU after the infection spread to his heart and lungs.

With his health failing, Charles contacted my church to ask if it would be possible for him to be baptized and forgiven for his sins. He was a deeply spiritual person, with a growing indignation at the apathy of the churches in the face of injustice around the globe. He was also increasingly drawn to Christian community, as described in the opening chapters of the Book of Acts.

A couple from our congregation went to visit him in the hospital. They spent days discussing the most important tenets of faith: repentance, confession, and forgiveness of sins. Charles felt that the greatest need of humankind was the need for forgiveness. Through those talks, Charles realized that he needed much greater compassion and understanding for his authoritarian father, who had been deeply wounded inwardly by his experiences during the Korean War. He also felt personal guilt for despairing of life in his most difficult moments.

After a few days, Charles was baptized. In the hospital room of such an ailing man, the words of Jesus became real: "It is not the healthy who need a doctor, but the sick...For I have not come to call the righteous, but sinners" (Matt. 9:12–13).

Charles eventually came to live in my community. Initially he was overwhelmed by being suddenly immersed in an environment brimming with people and activity, when he'd been used to a far more contemplative lifestyle. Even though he was at times independent and stand-offish, he seemed to grasp the importance of surrounding oneself with believers who could help each other during times of floundering. A few months later he told us:

Sometimes when I find myself feeling weighed down by sin, I start ransacking my soul and mind, and I come up with all kinds of excuses that act like an ointment or a salve on the wound. But the thing that's helped me most is a line from one of the Psalms. It's brought me comfort for many years. It just says, "Be still and know that I am God." When I let myself be still, I stop grabbing for the rope like a drowning person and just kind of let myself drown, and I find that I'm rescued – either directly, through God, or through another person that God sends along.

For quite a few years I really had been looking for some kind of community. But I think after I got sick, I wasn't looking for community as much as I was feeling very sorry for myself. I was tired of going back and forth to the hospital, and needing oxygen and medications, and not doing the stuff that I used to do. Suddenly I was just kind of scooped up out of the hospital and brought here. But I still wasn't really looking for community. I was looking for a place where I could make my peace with God and die.

After being here, even just for a few weeks, being around everybody, that started to change. I felt resentment about it changing, the way people were kind of getting to me. I still wanted to hold on firmly to my plan, just make peace with God and die because I couldn't do a lot of the things that I liked doing.

But finally, I just couldn't stand it anymore, trying to feel resentment or to push people away from me, and what I want to say is a very big "Sorry." There are things I can't do, but I've learned that there are so many new things I can do. If there has ever been a time in my life when it has been easier to see the face of Christ in the people that I'm around, it has been here. I want to live as long as possible.

Charles's story shows the importance of neighborhood and community. No matter how accomplished or independent we may once have been, when the realization of our declining faculties sets in, we should turn to others. Then we will find the purpose we so desperately need.

Combatting Loneliness

Vince and Jean DeLuca
"You're never too old to serve."

4

Finding Purpose

MOST PEOPLE think about the meaning of aging
or seek for purpose and resolution at the end of their
life. Many ask themselves, "How can I make my last
years more enjoyable, more exciting?" Wouldn't a
better question be, "How can God use my last days
to his purpose?"

Perhaps God can use us best when we give,
rather than receive. Old age provides many unique
opportunities to give, no matter what one's circumstances. I've seen, countless times, how people my
age do important things. I often think of the many
grandmothers holding families together and all
the grandfathers serving on boards or commit-
tees without pay. They spend many hours in service
at church, with their Rotary club or veterans'

organization, or the local soup kitchen – and often care for grandchildren while their own children are at work, unable to afford day care.

The simple services these people perform are invaluable, and not only in terms of what is produced; much of what the elderly contribute cannot be measured in dollars and cents. God never asks, "How much money did you make?" or "How successful were you?" or "How much influence did you have on people?" Nothing in life is more essential than giving and serving.

We can especially give to children, since we have the time to give a child personal attention. For example, with our wealth of knowledge of world history or some other subject, we could tutor a child who needs special help. My own children benefitted greatly from such help in subjects such as math and history.

Children are enriched through their contact with us, and even without realizing it or wanting it, we can become role models. These interactions do not need to be complex; my wife and I have found that sometimes all people need is someone to listen to them. But if we can do more, we should: when we take a child or teenager fishing or hiking, or to a ballgame or concert, we forge a friendship that will stay with that child for their entire life.

The apostle Paul says that one of our duties, as we get older, is to pass on wisdom to the next generation.

> Teach the older men to be temperate, worthy of respect, self-controlled, and sound in faith, in love, and in endurance…Similarly, encourage the young men to be self-controlled. In everything set them an example by doing what is good. In your teaching show integrity, seriousness, and soundness of speech that cannot be condemned, so that those who oppose you may be ashamed, because they have nothing bad to say about us. (Titus 2:2–8)

In recent years, I have made a greater effort to do this, spending more time with my grandchildren in hopes of influencing their lives positively. I've taught a number of them to drive, and the hours in the car, while nerve-wracking at times, provided many chances to share life experiences.

When one of my grandsons, Timothy, was in middle school, I invited him to join my wife and me on our morning walks, because I wanted to teach him to think critically. I'd forgotten the exact circumstances until he wrote about one of these excursions a few years later in a high school paper.

As we walked along, Opa made his case. He began by sounding very reasonable. "You know, Timothy, I think it is time you stopped keeping bees. They are a strain on your dad's time, they haven't given you much, and they are too much work for your family. I like honey, but from what I have seen, it isn't worth the price of hives or the expense and time for you to grow your own. Now, tell me what you think."

It was a warm spring day. I could hear the birds singing and smell wet asphalt after the morning rain. "Well, I've always enjoyed keeping bees. They make good honey. I like working with my dad. Uhhh... I don't know."

Then he got worked up. "What do you mean, you don't know? Use your brain! Think! I've just told you something you don't agree with. Now what are you going to say?"

I was wrecked. What was I supposed to do? Who argues with their grandfather, anyway? I looked at the ground.

"Well, what are you going to say?"

Just then I recalled something I'd once read about the significance of having pollinators around. "Opa, I read this essay ages ago. If I remember right, it said that if nobody kept bees, the world would end in seven years! Beat that!"

He was happy. "Holy cow, I didn't know that." But then he got serious. "Listen, Timothy. I'll tell you why I asked you this. I want you to grow up knowing how to think. You like to read, and that's awesome. But God gave you a head, and you need to learn how to use it. The way you will learn that is by communicating with others. Don't ever forget that."

I never did. We kept on walking, and Opa kept talking, his voice growing louder: "I don't think God even created bees! They are an invention of the devil! Tell me why God would create something with a sting!" I was a little nervous, but I heard my Oma chuckle, and as I looked up at Opa, I saw a twinkle in his eye.

Such encounters need to be treasured and are of value for the future. Ancient societies understood this better than we do. Kent Nerburn writes of a Native American elder who said:

If you see life as a straight line, where the young and old are weak and those in the middle are strong, and if you think that to be important you must be useful, you do not see value in the young and the old. You see them as burdens, not as gifts, because they cannot lift their hands to be of use to the community.

But the young and old both have other gifts...The old have the wisdom of experience. They have traveled far on the journey of life and give us knowledge about our own road ahead. They have lived what we are still waiting to learn...

Do you understand this, how the children are a gift to the elders and how the elders are a gift to the children? How they complete the circle of life like morning and evening complete the circle of the day?

Another valuable service we can provide is our experience with life's many difficult questions. The biblical figure Job asks, "Is not wisdom found among the aged? Does not long life bring understanding?" (Job 12:12). Youth may sometimes be marked by an aura of invincibility, but this is quickly shattered by failures and unfulfilled hopes. As young people embark on the journey of life and begin to hit rough patches, we can provide balance and reassurance. Whether they think so or not, people who have weathered many storms possess much wisdom.

Father Aldo Trento, a priest in Paraguay who works with the poor, has seen this firsthand.

> The greatness of old age is that it has wisdom, which is also important for young people. A young person who is about to face life has thousands of problems, but an old man can demystify many of these problems. If I have to go talk to someone, I go to an older person who will help me to understand and show me the way. If I would go to a young man, what could he tell me? He has no experience. Experience means not only doing but also judging. When I think of the elderly and their wisdom, they have experience and judgment, and that's why they say, "Son, this is the way. This is what's best for you." This for me is the essence of the old person: a companion for us in life.

We can also inspire the young by simple faithfulness, dedication, and enthusiasm in small things. Vince and Jean DeLuca are an elderly couple in a nearby town. I first met them at one of my son's high school football games, where they lent me an umbrella in an unexpected downpour. Vince played football for the school years ago, and he and Jean still attend every game. He is always there to encourage the players, thank them for their great efforts, cheer their victories, and stand by in their losses, while also reminding them that there is life after football.

Vince took over his family laundry business when his father died. His father taught him to work hard and always do his best for the customer. Until he was married he gave every check he earned to his father. On his wedding day, his father surprised him by giving him a bank book with all the money in it.

Vince and Jean continued running their business until a few years ago, when they were both in their eighties. It was always more than a laundry; it was a place where people could come to share their problems and find a listening ear, compassion, encouragement, and often material or financial support.

When I first met Vince, he was in his sixties, and I expressed surprise at the hours he worked. "Oh, I only work half time," he said. "I can hardly wait for each new day!" He got up at five o'clock each morning, went to work with a bag lunch, and only closed shop to return home again after five in the evening. For Vince, a twelve-hour day was a half-time job.

But Vince and Jean did not stop there. Now that they are no longer in business, they spend their days volunteering locally, mentoring younger volunteers and inspiring them to work hard in whatever vocation they might choose. As Vince and Jean get older and physically weaker, it seems they get spiritually stronger. In the end, their intelligence and success pale in comparison with the peace, simplicity, and quiet joy that they offer.

Vince and Jean don't need much care yet; they are still able-bodied. But when we do begin to need more help, we should remember this important point: by allowing others the chance to care for us, we can actually give to the givers. In doing so, we can be an anchor for them in times of storm. Jerome (not his real name), a home care provider for the elderly, found this out at a crucial juncture in his life.

I found fulfillment in my work, but my marriage was on the rocks. After much soul searching, my wife, Judy, decided to take our four children and leave me. We parted, possibly for good.

It was at this point that my daily home care visits to an older married couple I'll call Tom and Rose began to acquire a greater significance. Looking back, they were a godsend amidst the inner turmoil I was experiencing. I visited their home often, and we got to know one another very well. Their life had not been easy. Tom fought in World War II, but didn't want to talk about it. A retired stonemason, he was now diabetic and used a walker. Rose had suffered a stroke and was arthritic.

Until this point I had kept the relationship on a professional level. I did their laundry, helped them bathe, and occasionally cooked their dinner (they loved spicy Italian and Mexican foods). I was required to wear hospital scrubs at all times, which I did until Rose asked me if I could please show up at their house in jeans and T-shirt and be like one of their family; they didn't want a 'medic person' with them. Then they requested that I start joining them for meal-times, saying it didn't feel right to them otherwise. I told them about the company policy regarding the uniform, keeping it professional, and not accepting gifts from clients. Tom said, "Why don't you forget the agency. This is our house, not theirs. I make the rules in this house. You can consider yourself one of the family."

Naturally, they noticed something was wrong when my wife and children left me. They told me that when I was ready, they'd be there for me, and I could tell them whatever it was. At the dinner table that evening I told them that I was alone now and wasn't certain what the future held. They told me that they'd do their best to be sensitive during this difficult time. They asked about our marriage vows and told me about theirs: "Till death do us part." We had common ground there – my wife and I had promised the same. They believed that things would work out for us.

They recalled a rocky time early in their own marriage, which had nevertheless survived more than fifty years. They assured me that they would pray for Judy and me, which I know they did.

Eventually their prayer was answered. When I was finally able to reunite with Judy and the kids some months down the road, I remembered the time Tom and Rose cared for me, while I was ostensibly caring for them. Their faith in me and in God helped me more than I can say. I'll always remember the Bible passage Rose read to me on a particularly difficult day: "If our hearts condemn us, we know that God is greater than our hearts, and he knows everything" (1 John 3:20).

Perhaps the most important thing we can give, as old people, is prayer. Pope Benedict XVI spoke about this a few years ago at a home for the elderly in Rome. (I've met Benedict a number of times; at one meeting, before he was elected pope, he blessed my grandson Timothy).

At times, at a certain age, we may look back nostalgically at the time of our youth when we were fresh and planning for the future. Thus at times our gaze is veiled by sadness, seeing this phase of life as the time of sunset...Although I am aware of the difficulties that our age entails I would like to tell you with deep conviction: it is beautiful to be old!

Dear elderly brothers and sisters, though the days sometimes seem long and empty, with difficulties, few engagements, and few meetings, never feel down at heart: you are a wealth for society, even in suffering and sickness. And this phase of life is also a gift for deepening your relationship with God. Do not forget that one of the valuable resources you possess is the essential one of prayer: become interceders with God, praying with faith and with constancy. Pray for the church and pray for me, for the needs of the world, for the poor, so that there may be no more violence in the world. The prayers of the elderly can protect the world, helping it, perhaps more effectively than collective anxiety.

A few years ago, a neighboring church was struggling for a way to reach their young people. They set up "prayer buddies" for a year: an old person was paired up with a teenager. They did not meet; all they had was the name of another person to pray for every day. At the end of the year the church held a banquet at which the prayer buddies met. They told me they were amazed at how such a simple idea fostered a genuine, warm connection between young and old.

Sometimes such a program can lead to lasting friendships, but this is not always possible. Still, we can touch the heart of everyone we meet, no matter how brief the encounter. To paraphrase from a story my father wrote as a young man:

Why don't we use our time in a better way? Don't we know what a short time we have? The greatest gift

Finding Purpose

anyone has is a relationship with other people and with God. Each person should seek a true encounter with everyone he meets. By that I mean a real understanding of what is deepest in that person. Such an encounter does not vanish with time, which is fleeting. It stays with us; it has lasting value. Every person we meet is an opportunity to come closer to the truth.

If this is all we can do in our old age, it should be enough. This can be a difficult role to accept. Even Paul wrestled with wanting to die and be with Christ, yet also wanting to stay and help those on earth whom he knew and loved (Phil. 1:22–24). No matter how much time we have ahead of us, we should use it to lead others to a deeper, more prayerful relationship with God. This is perhaps the greatest gift we can give.

Winifred Hildel, a vibrant seventy-nine-year-old and long-time neighbor, had a fairly standard heart surgery. But complications arose, and she died suddenly in the hospital. What a shock for her family, who had expected her to return home within a few days. A few weeks later, her principal surgeon wrote this letter to her husband, Rudi, showing how Winifred's deep faith in Jesus affected the lives of many she came into contact with.

Thank you for taking the time from this most difficult period to remember me in your thoughts. Your letter is very important to me and helps me reaffirm that as a physician I do not make the final decision of life and death. It is the will of our God that guides each of us home.

Winifred was a delightful person. When I spoke with her it was clear that she was full of life and eager to share her enthusiasm for life with those around her. As she lay in the hospital with so many friends and family around her singing and praying, I knew she had touched so many souls, and I so wanted her to get well. I felt her loss would leave such an emptiness in those lives. Now I see that, though I am sure she is missed, she has left no emptiness behind. Instead she has left a legacy of joy, music, and love to you and your children. That makes her loss a bit more acceptable to me.

I cannot close without telling you how your faith and the faith of your family affected all of us at the hospital. Never before have we been witness to the expression of God's love and love for each other as we saw around Winifred's bed each day. We get tired and worn from the task of caring for the sick, and at times lose touch with our feelings. Many tears were shed in the unit when Winifred passed on – something that doesn't happen very often. They were shed because we were renewed and reminded why we were called to be there. Thank you for that renewal.

Even in dying, we can lead others to God. The way we live our lives and meet death can have a great effect on those who stay behind. Henry Ward Beecher once mused:

When the sun finally drops below the horizon in the early evening, evidence of its work remains for some time. The skies continue to glow for a full hour after its departure. In the same way, when a good or a great person's life comes to its final sunset, the skies of this world are illuminated until long after he is out of view. Such a person does not die from this world, for when he departs he leaves much of himself behind – and being dead, he still speaks.

Regardless of our age or health, none of us actually knows how much longer we will have to touch the lives of those around us. All the more, we should ask God to help us use our remaining strength for his purpose.

Christel Klüver
*"When you are with children
you become a child yourself again."*

5

Keeping Faith

As we grow older, we inevitably become more infirm. This brings with it discomfort and frustration, then physical pain and mental anguish. Nobody likes to suffer; we all do our best to avoid it. But in this world there is simply a lot of suffering and much sin. We cannot escape it. After all, Adam and Eve, after they disobeyed God, were sent from the Garden of Eden with the promise of a life of suffering for them and their descendants (Gen. 3:16–19).

If we try too strenuously to avoid illness and pain, we will miss out on an important aspect of aging: the redemptive power of suffering. One aspect of this power is the way our own suffering can open us to the suffering of others. Another is the way suffering can turn us to God.

Undergoing suffering can be compared to gold being refined in a fire, preparing us for our ultimate goal, which is to be fully united with God. The Quaker theologian Thomas R. Kelly, whose writings influenced a number of my friends in their search for Jesus, understood this deeply:

> The heart is stretched through suffering, and enlarged. But O the agony of this enlarging of the heart, that one may be prepared to enter into the anguish of others!...The cross as dogma is painless speculation; the cross as lived suffering is anguish and glory. Yet God, out of the pattern of his own heart, has planted the cross along the road of holy obedience. And he enacts in the hearts of those he loves the miracle of willingness to welcome suffering and to know it for what it is – the final seal of his gracious love.

If suffering does not lead us to God, it will lead to despair and hopelessness. Viktor Frankl, the Austrian psychiatrist who spent three years in Auschwitz, discovered what he thought was the biggest killer of people: a loss of hope. Frankl noticed that when even a fit person lost hope or a reason to live, he succumbed quickly:

The prisoner who had lost his faith in the future – his future – was doomed. With his loss of belief in the future, he also lost his spiritual hold; he let himself decline and became subject to mental and physical decay. Usually this happened quite suddenly, in the form of a crisis, the symptoms of which were familiar to the experienced camp inmate. We all feared this moment – not for ourselves, which would have been pointless, but for our friends.

In a similar way, Friedrich Nietzsche noted that he who has a "why" to live can endure any "how." I have counseled many who lack this "why" – this purpose. Living in hell and seeing no way out, they are tempted by thoughts of suicide or euthanasia, or as it is euphemistically named, "death with dignity."

Yet even if compassion is the motivation, the taking of any human life is wrong. God created each of us "in the image of God." Since he gave us life, only he has the right to end it. Suicide is a form of rebellion against God, a statement that says, "I am beyond hope. My problem is too big for even God to handle." Suicide denies that God's grace is greater than our weakness.

If we find ourselves in such a situation, we can always seek God and ask for his compassion and mercy. Even when we are at the end of our rope, God wants to give us new hope and courage, no matter how deeply we feel we may have betrayed him. God is ready to forgive every sin. We only need to be humble enough to ask him. When someone is tempted by thoughts of suicide, the most important thing we can do is to show that person love, to remind him that he, and each one of us, was created by God and that we each have a purpose to fulfill.

It can be frightening, but also rewarding, to help someone through suicidal depression. Take Hugo Stahel, a man I knew from childhood, and in many ways, a second father to me. Hugo was a tall, hard-working man, but the hardships he suffered in life almost brought him down. His oldest son committed suicide at the age of twenty-nine. This devastated Hugo and his wife and tormented him for the rest of his life.

In his last years Hugo suffered from many ailments, physical and spiritual. He lost his wife. He struggled with suicidal thoughts and even made some attempts.

I spent many hours listening to him, reminding him that his family and all who knew and loved him would be devastated by his death. Hugo had a strong faith, but he often doubted the presence of God. He doubted that he could be forgiven for trying to end his life. But as his physical strength waned, his faith grew; in the end, prayer and love seemed to overcome everything else. Hugo died peacefully at the age of eighty-seven.

Suicide and euthanasia are the most drastic measures we human beings take to avoid suffering. Yet even if we never entertain such thoughts, we often do our best to avoid suffering at all costs. Too often, when faced with a medical situation, as many of us are, we turn only to professionals, rather than asking ourselves, "What does God want of me?" or "What is God saying to me through this problem?" Fear of serious illness or death certainly plays a role, and perhaps in many of us there is more fear than we dare to admit. If only we could free ourselves of this fear and focus on God!

Medicine plays a significant role in the lives of most elderly people, but it can be just as much a curse as a blessing. Over-medicalizing old age can be dehumanizing, and those who agree to every last test or diagnostic procedure are opening a Pandora's Box. "Problems" are discovered that aren't really problems at all; that is, they are conditions a person may have died with, but not from. And once a doctor finds these problems, he is obligated to deal with them. Now the slippery slope begins, where each test leads to another. Sooner or later, one of these interventions may prove fatal, by way of infection, surgical complication, or drug interaction.

We should ask ourselves if we aren't being hoodwinked by medical science. These days, practically every organ in the body can be replaced or repaired, and plenty of good arguments are advanced in favor of doing so. But let us not forget that in the not-too-distant past, people lived and died without much medical attention at all. Though their life expectancy was shorter, they lived fruitful and productive lives, perhaps more so than we do today.

Throughout my childhood, Christel Klüver and her family were close neighbors. Her brothers were some of my best friends; they stuck with me through bad as well as good times. An energetic kindergarten teacher, Christel was stricken with multiple sclerosis in her early forties. This slowly changed her from an active, capable woman to one who had to rely more and more on medicine. The drugs may have helped, but eventually she felt they might be hindering her from living a more fulfilled life. One of her caregivers remembers:

When I came to care for Christel, she had no control over her lower body. She was experiencing spasms and pain, and was starting to lose her drive to keep mentally and spiritually active. This had been her most outstanding characteristic before the disease struck. She was taking many drugs. They helped to counter the basic problems, but had numerous side effects. She was losing her memory and her sense of time and chronology.

She began to wonder: Have I put more faith in medicine than in God? She decided to reduce or eliminate all but one or two drugs and treatments. It was not an easy decision, and we struggled with her over the prospects of an unknown outcome. It was a step in faith.

Amazingly enough, Christel turned a corner. She continued to have some spasms, but they were less frequent than before. She became more wakeful, more alert, her conversation broader and livelier. There had been much prayer for her situation, and she had fought inner battles as well as bearing the disease. We will never forget this miracle of healing of a different nature than we would have imagined. In spite of her illness, Christel radiated joy and love for the rest of her life.

Some years ago, I experienced something that made me reconsider my reliance on medicine and medical professionals. I went for a routine cardiac checkup and was told I needed major heart surgery. Not only that; they told me they needed to operate immediately. I had no time to prepare.

After the surgery, there were several days when I believed that I would not pull through. There were moments when I didn't know if I would ever see my family and friends again. But the staff let my wife and me have precious time together. For the first time in a long while, we asked ourselves, "Are we really ready to be separated? What if we don't see one another tomorrow?" It was redeeming to be able to ask each other for forgiveness. We cried a lot together, and we also laughed a lot.

Thankfully, the outcome of that surgery was positive, although I have not made a complete recovery. At that time, I often listened to Mendelssohn's *Elijah,* the story of one of God's great prophets. One aria struck me quite personally: "Commit thy way unto him and trust in him." It is hard to actually submit to God. It goes against human nature. We rebel and resist, because it means giving up control and dismantling our personal power.

At the time of this ordeal, I remembered the Old Testament figure of Job. Here was a man who had everything the world prizes: wife, property, children, success, and status. But God allowed Satan to test Job, to see if he would still love God without earthly riches. He soon lost everything, even his health. His friends, and even his wife, mocked him and told him to curse God. But because he praised God and submitted to his will, everything was eventually restored to him in even greater measure.

My heart is still not healthy. Doctors could offer me another open heart surgery with valve replacements, and I might live another ten or twenty years – but I'm not going to go that route. Instead, I'm going to work for God's kingdom until my valves give out and then I'm going to sing praises to God. If I try to prolong my life because I am scared to die, what will I gain? It doesn't matter if I live only one more day, or ten more years; it must all be to his praise and glory.

Dick Domer

"The world's gonna have to take care of itself now!"

6

Living with Dementia

Though the aches and pains of old age usually start out as mere inconveniences, they soon assume more serious proportions. It is the same with the breaking down of our minds: what starts as ordinary forgetfulness and absentmindedness often progresses into the ravages of dementia, the most common form of which is Alzheimer's. This disease has been increasingly on my mind, as several beloved members of my church have been stricken with it in recent years.

For most (if not all) of us, the prospect of losing our minds is nothing short of terrifying. But perhaps that's because we as a society are approaching it all wrong. Maybe people would fear it less if they didn't have to worry so much about becoming confined to a ward in a nursing home. Perhaps we need to value and cherish those afflicted by this disease, rather than institutionalize them. In my church we attempt to integrate them into congregational life and activities as much as possible. Younger members take turns helping to care for them on weekends or just spend time with them.

A disorder such as Alzheimer's needs to be faced with patience and love in a family setting wherever possible. It can be difficult, but the alternative is much worse. The way people with dementia are warehoused in long-term care units is something I wouldn't wish for anyone, especially a loved one. On the other hand, countless families have no other choice than to send their parents to such a facility. No wonder they feel guilt, pain, and shame for having to do so. Yet there is no simple solution to such need. Or is there?

As hard as it may be, I often wonder what would happen if, as a society, we chose to focus more on the positive aspects of the disease: the return to childlikeness. People suffering from dementia can be a treasure, not only a burden. Alzheimer's does not need to be an experience of shame, misery, and hell for those involved. As Detlef Manke, a pastor who worked with Alzheimer's patients in Germany, told me:

> If somebody wants to learn how to serve, let them care for somebody who has Alzheimer's. If somebody wants to learn compassion, let them be with people who have Alzheimer's, because there is nothing more wonderful and rewarding than to receive their love when you make them feel understood in every regard.
>
> They also teach us to live fully in the present – this in itself can be an adventure. They may be sad or aggravated one moment, and the next moment everything is wonderful. The caregiver has to be ready to answer the same question every few minutes.
>
> And always, they need to be respected as personalities rich in years and experience. If we think they talk nonsense, it is we who are stupid; we just do not have the key to their rich world.
>
> Only those who find this key will experience the so-called "windows" that open even at the very last stages of Alzheimer's. These windows open right onto eternity. Having experienced this again and again over the years, I am convinced that, at the deepest level, a person's spirit cannot be touched by the disease.

As Detlef suggests, rather than trying to help an Alzheimer's patient make sense of our world, we should try to understand theirs. Of course, knowing this does not necessarily make it easy to do. A member of my church gave me some insight into the matter. When her father-in-law developed dementia, it progressed rapidly, and it wasn't pretty.

> The disease evidenced itself in all kinds of unusual behavior. He would disappear from his house, and his caregiver would follow and try to bring him back, but it was very difficult to reason with him. He was beset by the conviction that people were plotting against him and would sometimes spend three or four hours prowling around in his bedroom looking in cupboards and under furniture with a flashlight to see if anyone was hiding there. He became violent at times, even towards his elderly wife. He resisted attempts to help him with his personal hygiene. During an attempt at a shower, he punched my husband's nose so violently that he thought his father had broken it. In his last weeks, he refused to go to bed and would sit up in his recliner all night. His caregiver's attempts at persuading him to take off his shoes and go to bed were futile.

To see our father go through such torment brought us to our knees in prayer. We were so helpless in trying to care for him because of his energetic resistance. We could only go through one day at a time and try not to look too far into the future. We had to remind ourselves again and again that this was not the husband and father that we knew and loved, but someone suffering from a mental illness just as people suffer from physical illness.

Through all the storms, my mother-in-law stood firm to her promise to stick with her husband until death should part them. She never stopped hoping that things would get better. Her faithfulness and hopefulness were a tremendous witness to us.

My father-in-law's life came to an end fairly suddenly. He refused all medication and then all food and drink. He then went into a coma and died soon after. After he had gone, we could only echo the words of Martin Luther King Jr.: "Free at last, free at last, thank God Almighty: he's free at last."

Wherever we are given the grace to find such patience as the woman just quoted, we will discover great blessings in it. For one thing, we will have our eyes opened to something Detlef referred to, above: the way a person with dementia often lives and moves in another world.

Rebekah, a family friend, experienced this first-hand with her father, Dick Domer, a brilliant man I've known since I was in high school. Dick's grasp of politics, business, and social issues, as well as his wit and humor, made him an exciting person to be with. But when Alzheimer's struck, things changed for him and for the family. Rebekah told me:

> The early stages were the worst because most people didn't believe that anything was wrong with Dad. He could be so sharp and witty, and he could remember facts and figures flawlessly. But we were increasingly aware that his brain was deteriorating. Mom and I felt the change most keenly as we were closest to him. It reached a point where Dad had to stop driving and then leave his office job.
>
> I worried that Dad would be humiliated by these changes, but he humbly accepted them. He let Mom and me assist him at home, accepting our reminders thankfully (most of the time). Instead of becoming bitter and frustrated, Dad found new outlets in life that fulfilled him in a wonderful way. He also didn't

lose his humor. One day we ate Dove chocolate and were reading the messages. Mine said, "Relax your mind." Dad answered, "That is, if you have one!"

He spent more time with Mom, often sitting out under the trees, reading and visiting with anyone passing by. He smoked his pipe while she knitted. He played with his grandchildren, reading to them and listening to their tales of adventure at the end of the day. Our family gathered most summer evenings around a campfire to sing American folk songs. Both my parents were musical, and Dad loved the old American songs of pioneering like "Home on the Range."

It seemed that Dad's love to us deepened. He became softer and more compassionate. He depended on us more, and he appreciated our help. But most of all, he drew on the deep faith in Jesus that had been the core of his life for so many years.

One by one, Dad was robbed of his abilities. Previously an avid croquet player, the day came when he couldn't figure out how the game worked anymore. I played chess with him until that too became too difficult to understand. We then tried Scrabble. For a while, that worked, even if Dad spelled his words backwards or upside down. But then he realized, with tears in his eyes, "No, I can't do that anymore...it's a lot of nonsense."

After Mom died, it became a real challenge to find meaningful ways to occupy Dad as his disease progressed. I spent many hours taking short walks with him. He loved nature and always enjoyed meeting children along the road. I took him black-berry picking along the paths. We sat out every evening watching the sun set as he smoked his pipe and talked to me about Mom, about his spiritual search for life's meaning as a young man, and about his childhood experiences. I heard the same stories hundreds of times, but it didn't matter. We were together. He was happy with me at his side, listening to whatever he could still recall. He was most peaceful when we just accepted him as he was, without making him do things he could no longer enjoy. We learned to accept his reality and stop expecting him to understand ours.

How can we find joy and blessings when confronted with the daily realities of seeing our loved ones change so drastically? How can we see the positives when so much of our experience is confusion, anger, and perhaps even violence? Johann Christoph Blumhardt, a nineteenth-century German pastor, wrote:

> When you suffer tribulation, keep in mind that you must do so in such a way that it is not just a victory for yourself but a victory over suffering in general. I have experienced this among epileptics, among the blind, the lame, and the deaf, and in general among the so-called incurably sick. I tell them: Be glad that you are like this. Now bring something of Jesus' death and his resurrection into your situation...Then you will help to gain a victory for the whole world...
>
> Do not fear, even if you suffer in spirit and have to realize how weak you are. The Risen One can so permeate your weakness that you can be more alive than many proud people who, with all their health and strength, blithely and proudly prance through life. When you have to bear sickness, especially one that is humanly incurable, stand still, reflect, and remember the one who died and came to life.

Jesus provides an answer to every need, and God knows what is in every heart, even if we don't. Ultimately, Jesus can and will use us, even if our minds and bodies are broken and decaying.

Carole Neal
"The best way to face death is to really live."

7

Moving Forward

WE'VE ALL KNOWN OLDER PEOPLE who vow to keep fighting until the end rather than slipping into passive decline. On the whole, it's an excellent attitude. It seems like every few years we read a story of the "101-year-old marathon runner." But what about when, despite resolutions, we're forced to slow down? Martin Luther King Jr., with whom I marched in the Civil Rights movement in the 1960s, encouraged his supporters in this way: "If you can't fly, run; if you can't run, walk; if you can't walk, crawl, but by all means keep moving."

Carole Neal was an example of someone who put these words into practice. She amazed everyone who knew her by the way she kept herself moving, even in the face of an aggressive terminal cancer. On the one hand, this emotionally fragile woman was filled with fear; on the other, she had the confidence of someone who knew she possessed the right weapons for the battle facing her:

I'll be honest: when "the time comes," I hope no one starts singing those hymns about floating around in heaven. I'd think I was already descending into my grave. You know, the words of those songs may be deep, but for some reason, hearing them sung reminds me of all the most depressing things in life. I know it shouldn't be that way, but it is. I need energy, strength for the fight for life. And I can get that straight from the Gospels.

I start each day by reading the Gospels, and Jesus – this most radical, revolutionary lover of *life* – absolutely blows my mind every time I read his words. He had this unheard-of compassion for the weak and sinful, yet he shouted at the strong and powerful (though he loved them as well), and he had a deep reverence for God, his Father, our Father. But he wasn't pious. I'll bet he had a whale of a time in everything he did.

Now you're going to think this is weird, but to me the battle has been like an adventure, the adventure of my life: the necessity of fighting something that is absolutely deadly. I felt from the beginning that I wasn't going to let any part of this disease take me over. And I didn't want to hear about suffering; I didn't want to know about dying; I didn't want to read about heaven and angels and all that kind of thing.

But in reading through the Gospels, I feel I've gotten a really good picture of Jesus. To me, *that* is where life is. Jesus fought every evil and loved everyone, without reservation; with compassion, but with incredible straightforwardness. Not that I could ever do that. But that's how I've wanted to live my life – with that kind of fervor.

It's always good to maintain a fighting attitude, as Carole did. However, clinging to one's independence doesn't always yield happiness. I know of several cases where dying people made life difficult for themselves and others by holding on to their independence at all costs, or who were overwhelmed by life simply because they couldn't accept the realities of the aging process. Perhaps that was because they feared that giving in to old age meant some sort of passive defeat. But I think there is an important difference between "letting go" and "giving up."

In one of his most memorable poems, William Blake equates hanging on to life and its admitted richness with destroying a beautiful butterfly as we admire it too closely.

> He who binds to himself a joy
> Does the wingéd life destroy;
> But he who kisses the joy as it flies
> Lives in eternity's sunrise.

As Blake says, we can easily extinguish something of God by grasping it too tightly to ourselves. We want to keep living the way we've always been living, because it is familiar, comfortable, and in many cases, beautiful. But that can prevent us from deeply experiencing our life as God wants us to. My older sister Roswith Mason dealt with this, and it was not easy. First she had to let go of a ten-year-old daughter who died of osteosarcoma. Some twenty years later, she was diagnosed with cancer. Only weeks later, her husband, Dave, was discovered to have cancer as well. In six months, he was gone. In her words:

When you are young, you don't ponder the possibility of death – at least I didn't. You're just full of life and energy, full of ideas about the future. But having cancer has made me face my mortality. It has meant I have had to submit to others, to realize I'm not as physically capable as I once was. Through that, I've learned a lot about humility.

In the years since Dave died, I have put up a fight against illness – I do not believe in giving up – but every step of the way, I've been learning to let go. I had always been an independent sort of person, able to manage and do all the little practical things that are part of running a household. But with Dave gone and my sickness taking hold, I had to accept that I was simply going to have to let others do things for me I would naturally have done for myself.

I've always been a middle-school teacher and love being with kids in and out of the classroom, but suddenly I just didn't have the stamina for that anymore. I had always assumed I would stay actively involved in the things I loved – teaching history, sewing, gardening – for as long as I could. Now I had to accept playing a supporting role. I had to let go, again and again, and make conscious decisions not to value myself in terms of how much I was contributing to others around me.

Amazingly, this got easier! It's not a big issue anymore. I have had wonderful chances in life, and now I have to give younger ones their turn. My involvement isn't so important; the world will turn without me. I simply have to submit to God's will and to the people around me who love and care for me.

I can understand how someone might find this submitting hard. It was for me, too, at first. But I know how much I have to be thankful for. I have had a blessed life, in spite of some trying times and in spite of making many mistakes. And I have the joy of being surrounded by my family and others who love me so much.

Two years after my initial cancer diagnosis, I found out I had breast cancer as well. On top of that, I started getting bouts of pneumonia. I was taking lots of medication, stronger and stronger prescriptions. It got to a point where I had to stop and confront the question, "Where is this going? What is God's will in all of this?"

Through praying about it and talking it over with my children and with friends I trust, I recognized that I needed to entrust my life to God. I decided that while I would continue to take medication to help control cancer-related pain, I would stop taking aggressive treatments to try to curb the pneumonia. Instead, I would rely on prayer and the support of those I love to see me through – whatever "through" might mean.

This was not an easy decision. I wanted a balance between saying "no" to more medicine and simply "giving up." I knew if I had a recurrence of pneumonia, my body was in poor shape to combat it on its own. But the amazing thing is, since making my decision I have had several bouts of pneumonia, and each time God has helped me through. I am still here, and I sure haven't given up.

Each time, I've had to fight through to find peace in the face of the question, Am I ready if this is the end? But I have been able to accept whatever God has in mind for me. This has given me the inner peace to know that things happen in God's hour, and to pray, as Jesus himself did, "Yet not as I will, but as you will" (Matt. 26:39).

Many of us don't want to let go. Yet Jesus says, "Whoever wants to save their life will lose it, but whoever

loses their life for me will find it" (Matt. 16:25).
Letting go means putting your life into God's hands
and living on his terms. Then if God gives the strength
to go on, we should give it all we have. When life no
longer depends on our efforts, we find peace and can
accept that God may have other plans, as Roswith has.

By letting go of our will, of all that could have been
and should have been, and by entrusting our failures
and mistakes into the hands of God, we can move
forward into our remaining years ready to do his will.
These can then be rewarding and meaningful – full of
gratitude and joy, rather than anxiety and worry. To
quote Henri Nouwen in this vein:

> You are still afraid to die. Maybe that fear is connected
> with some deep unspoken worry that God will not
> accept you as his. The question "Why do I have to
> die?" is connected to this fear. You asked it as a little
> child, and you are still asking it…God called you from
> the moment you were knitted together in your moth-
> er's womb (Psalm 139). It is your vocation to receive
> that love, and to give it back. From the very beginning
> you have, like every human being, experienced the
> forces of death. Whether physically (through aging

and illness) or inwardly (through temptation or sin) these forces have attacked you – through all your years of growing up – and they will continue to attack you. But even though you have often felt overwhelmed, you have been faithful. Hang on to that. Know that the dark forces will have no final power over you.

In a nutshell, this is the secret: to be faithful, and to hang on. If we do this, we will find that it actually doesn't matter how long we live; God is more concerned that we simply serve him and trust him to the very end. For the true measure of time is not found in years, but in living in accordance with our primary purpose here on earth: to love others.

Herbert Rogers, a street preacher in Kingston, New York, whom I met only near the end of his life, exemplified the idea that "how" we grow old is far more important than how "old" we grow. As the saying goes, "It's not the years in the life but the life in the years that matters." Although Herbie, as we called him, only reached fifty years of age, he accomplished more than most of us will in many more years.

At his funeral, Herbie was remembered not only as a brother, husband, and father, but also as a pastor, peacemaker, friend, and advocate to people his own family didn't even know. Even the local police and district attorney, who had arrested him hundreds of times, paid their respects; for Herbie had left a life of drugs, guns, and several years in prison to embrace a very practical ministry of service to others. As he rejoiced in his own redemption, he insisted that the lives of others could be restored and redeemed, too.

Herbie never passed up opportunities to remind his listeners just who had turned his life around. It was back in 1995, and he had knelt down on the floor of his prison cell, asking Jesus to come into his life: "If you're everything I've heard you are, come into my life and change me!" he recalled crying out. From then on, he moved in one direction only. To him, no soul was too broken for God to fix, no worn-out prostitute or shivering addict too far-gone to save. And so he carried his message of new life into the places no one else wanted to go: the county jail and state prisons, hospitals and homeless shelters, garbage-strewn lots and back alleys.

When, at fifty, he was diagnosed with untreatable cancer, his reaction was not unpredictable: though in pain and worried for the future of his family, he made it clear that he was not going to spend his last weeks in a hospital. There were tears, and even anger, but he never doubted for a minute that he was going home to God, and this stubborn faith held him through to the end. "It's not about me," he once said, already on his sickbed. "It's simply about getting God's work done."

Herbie's life shows that it is never too late to change, to give, to share, and to contribute. In the parable of the workers in the vineyard, those who came and worked hard for just an hour received the same pay as those who worked all day (Matt. 20:1–16). In Jesus' eyes, it's the very act of commitment, not the length of the commitment, that matters. Whether we begin to serve and love early or late in life, there are always opportunities to do so, no matter how sick or weak we are.

Herbert Rogers
"No soul is too broken to fix."

8

Finding Peace

For most people, there comes a time when we realize that our days are drawing to an end. We all wish to die peacefully, but how do we find this peace? True peace requires effort. Sometimes old hurts or past grudges are deeply buried in our subconscious, but they are still there, separating us from other people. We can choose to let these sleeping dogs lie, or we can choose to confront them. The first choice is certainly easier, but I have found that those who take the harder path often end up better equipped to face their future. They're not weighed down by burdens of the past. Sadly, too many people never experience this, spending their last years in bitterness. I have seen the lives of the most beautiful people ruined because they could not forgive.

Growing older should be a time to right old wrongs. This requires humility and forgiveness. Jesus tells us to be willing to forgive someone "seventy times seven" times if necessary (Matt. 18:22). He also tells us to forgive others so that we ourselves can be forgiven (Matt. 6:14). For many, the hardest thing can be to forgive oneself. But the rewards are immense. All of a sudden, you will feel like a human being again; you will be able to feel the needs of others.

Of course, this is important throughout our lives, but it is even more so as we prepare for the hour of death. Those who are confident of having received forgiveness for their sins, and of having forgiven those who have hurt them, can be spared much mental anguish in their final hours. We may still go through great physical torment, but we will be granted the peace of Jesus, perhaps in a way quite different from what we imagine. As Jesus himself said, "My peace I give you. I do not give to you as the world gives" (John 14:27). When we receive peace, we can then share it with others.

Rachel (not her real name), a Jewish woman from our neighborhood, was dying of cancer. She was seventy years old and had been a family and marriage counselor for years. In her work, she had helped many people find reconciliation by listening to them and offering advice. Yet Rachel now found herself lacking the very peace she had sought to give. As her cancer progressed and the end of her life drew near, she did not want to die alone, unsettled and with unresolved problems. Specifically, she knew she desperately needed to forgive her brother, to whom she had not talked in many years. She also told me, "You know, something else I have to do is to forgive my mother. She was jealous of me, of all the opportunities I had. She had to uproot and reinvent herself three times and give up a lot of her plans. I see now that it took a courageous woman to experience what she did in her life, with all that was happening in history."

Members of my church offered to care for Rachel during her last days. My wife and I visited her often. I was humbled that she called me her "Chief Rabbi," even though I am not Jewish. As we sat with her, she told us about her life, especially the toughest moments, when she had struggled with thoughts of suicide.

One evening, Rachel suddenly lifted up both hands as if she wanted to pray. She whispered very quietly, "I want to pray a prayer of gratefulness." She asked, "Do you think I will go tonight? I think I will. I prayed not to die alone. This has been granted to me."

A few days before Rachel died, her brother came, and they very simply forgave each other. After that she was ready to let go of everything; she had found peace.

As I found with Rachel and many others, what we need most is to be reassured that our sins are forgiven. Then there is no need to fear that moment when we will come before our Maker.

If we don't reconcile with those we've hurt and forgive those who've hurt us, we will find it very difficult to leave this world. Ben Zumpe, a cousin of mine, dealt with this very question. Ben was an unquenchable optimist, a passionate man who loved life. Yet within days of being diagnosed with a late-stage cancer, he accepted that he was going to die, most likely in a few months. One thing haunted him: his estrangement from his sons, who by this time were grown men and not living at home. Years before, they had painfully parted ways. Since then, attempts to mend the relationship had proved fruitless. Now Ben told me, "The last thing I want is that when I'm dead my boys feel their father had a grudge against them. I want to make it very clear to them that we as parents love them, and that we still pray for them."

So Ben wrote his sons a letter. It was difficult, and he put it off a number of times before finally finishing it. On the one hand, he yearned to make peace, realizing he too had made mistakes. Yet he also believed that, precisely because he loved his sons, he needed to be candid. His letter read, in part:

My dearly beloved children,

I write this letter with deep love to each of you, because I have cancer and am actually on my death-bed. I do not know how many days, weeks, or months I still have left. In other words, I do not know how long it will be before God takes me. All the more, my heart reaches out to you in the longing that you find Jesus. He came to this earth to spread a new gospel, so that every man can find redemption and new life – eternal life – through him. But following him means taking up the battle between good and evil, light and darkness, God and Satan.

Beloved children, as I already told you, I am now on my deathbed. I want you to know that I pray for you and that I love you. Have you forgotten, for example, how many times I reached out to each one of you when you were in college? But I also want you to know how painful it is for me that we cannot speak face to face. After all, I have invited each of you, at one time or another, to come back and see me. That offer still stands. It is never too late to find forgiveness on both sides. Turn to God. Turn to life. It is a matter of living for the good Spirit.

You should know, by the way, that I write to you from the depths of my heart. I do not want to be judgmental or to put you under any kind of pressure. Jesus wants voluntary followers, not people who follow him out of fear. Still, each of us will have to face the Creator one day. It is in this sense that I have written you this letter.

Ben sent off the letter with much trepidation. Remarkably, each of his sons responded positively. One by one, over the next months, they visited Ben and made peace. They asked their father for forgiveness, and he asked for theirs.

In the last days of Ben's life, I visited him every evening. We had grown up together and were very close. At this point, there was not much more to do than simply enjoy a shot of brandy and thank God for the reconciliation he had experienced. We laughed a lot and cried a lot.

Ben's death was one of the most difficult I have experienced. Near the end, his body was wracked with spasms. Unable to speak, Ben still communicated with his eyes as we wiped his brow with cool cloths. But I knew that in spite of great physical pain, he had faith that God was near him. Ben knew that what was perhaps even more important than the forgiveness he found with his sons was the forgiveness we each are offered by God, through the sacrifice of Jesus. A few weeks before he died, he told me:

> If it weren't for Jesus, who suffered and died on the cross for me, I couldn't face death. But Jesus suffered on Golgotha and experienced God-forsakenness, and he did that for me. I know that what Jesus suffered was a thousand times more than I can ever suffer because all the demons of the earth were trying to knock him out and attack him. But on the third day

he arose. I believe in the resurrection, and I believe in the forgiveness of sins.

Ben's story warms the heart. But what of difficult situations, where the dying person is divorced or separated? What of estranged families, abandoned parents, and broken relationships? Can we find peace here, too, even when reconciliation may seem impossible? I believe we can, but again, it has to start with forgiveness. Just as dying people need to forgive, they may also need to be forgiven – and by forgiving them, we allow them to go.

Charles Williams is the former police chief of a small town. I have known him for years; he frequently accompanies me to public schools to talk about non-violence and forgiveness, and how these can solve many of our interpersonal problems.

But he didn't always believe it himself. In fact, he only heard my program because he was at my presentation at his town's high school in his law enforcement capacity. But gradually, the idea of forgiveness worked in his heart, and now he tells his story almost weekly, hoping to change other lives.

Charles grew up in an alcoholic household. As he tells it, his mother didn't just have a drink now and then: her job was drinking. He was traumatized as a child, witnessing the fights between his parents. A particular image burned into his mind is of his father holding on to his mother's coat and her struggling to wriggle out of it and run out of the house, shouting, "Stop the world, I want to get off!" He remembers sitting at the dinner table trying to be a "good little boy" and eat his supper, with tears rolling down his cheeks, as this scene was re-enacted almost daily. He would come downstairs the next morning and find her passed out on the sofa, with cigarette burns on the carpet, and think how close the house had come to burning down.

Looking back, Charles realizes that for thirty years he had harbored a great hatred towards his mother – a hatred that affected every area of his life and caused him to make very bad choices. He became so desperate that when handed his gun upon graduation from the Police Academy, he seriously considered committing suicide.

After speaking more with me about the power of forgiveness, Charles visited his mother in his boyhood home. He sat across from her at the very table that was the scene of so many bad memories, and forgave her. Charles remembers, "It was as if the weight of a large knapsack I had been carrying for years fell from my shoulders. At that instant, my mother changed from being the fire-breathing dragon I remembered from my childhood to the frail, sick, elderly woman she was – the mother I never really had."

A few years later Charles sat at her bedside in a hospital as she was dying and wept as he told her again of his love and forgiveness. Although she had not moved for days, she put her hand on his, consoling him with her mother love.

"Had I not forgiven her, I could never have experienced that," Charles told me. "It is never the wrong time to do the right thing. Don't waste years harboring grudges, anger, and hatred as I did. Listen to the small voice of conscience and forgive, even if it's the last thing you want to do."

Facing death is easier when we have lived a life of service to others. In *The Brothers Karamazov,*

Dostoyevsky recounts the story of an old woman living in fear of death "to the point of suffering, terror, and fright." She pleads with Father Zossima to convince her about life after death. Father Zossima replies that such certainty comes only from love.

> Try to love your neighbors actively and tirelessly. The more you succeed in loving, the more you'll be convinced of the existence of God and the immortality of your soul. And if you reach complete selflessness in the love of your neighbor, then undoubtedly you will believe, and no doubt will even be able to enter your soul. This has been tested. It is certain.

Another crucial tool to finding peace is confessing. This is one of the hardest, but also one of the best things we can do, because it frees our hearts from fear and fills us with love, first of all to Jesus and then towards other people. Confessing is not just for Catholics. Find a trusted pastor, confidant, or even your spouse or an adult child with whom you can speak freely. Being able to talk about mistakes we've made or sins we've committed and now regret can free us from their burden and turn them into bygones. Of course, we don't need to wait until we're old to do this. The blessing of confession can be given at any time.

I experienced the peace that confession and forgiveness bring to a dying person while working with Richard Scott, a fellow elder in my church. He and I ministered to many dying people. But I never thought I would personally do the same for him. Richard was diagnosed with aggressive cancer when he was just sixty-one. He and his wife, Kathy, had a large family and weighty responsibilities in our church. He underwent surgery, yet within nine months of his diagnosis, he was dead.

Although Richard did not consider himself old, the way he used his last days was a challenge to all of us who knew him. Countless times, he pointed those he met to a life of service to others and Christ. He was no saint, but he found peace by confiding with fellow pastors, and by making a sincere effort to clear up any misunderstandings he had with members of our church.

At a certain point Richard made a decision to forgo further medical intervention. After initial struggles over this, the decision brought him and Kathy great peace in his last days.

To me, it is not the length of time I have but how it is used. I believe that after this experience of putting everything into God's hands, the gospel will become a lot more living and real. My situation has forced me to reflect on what it means to turn to God and totally trust him. It has also been very humbling to experience how many people, some of whom I hardly know, are praying for me. What a comfort it is when people care for one another; this has provided me the most support.

In the parable of the unjust judge, Jesus points out that this battle takes hard work. The widow had to go again and again to the judge. Finally he got fed up and gave her what she wanted (Luke 18:1–5). Of course, God doesn't respond to us because he gets fed up with us – he actually loves us – but he also wants us to work at things. He doesn't always just give; sometimes he wants to see if we really want what we are asking for.

I do not want to ask for a longer life. It has been shown very clearly to me in these days how very insignificant and unimportant my life is. If God wants me to live longer, I will – no question. If he doesn't,

I won't. What is a far greater gift is how we can encourage each other, instead of wallowing in sadness and discouragement. I want to use whatever time I have left to point people to God's kingdom.

There is a longing in every heart to find peace. What I have been grappling with more than anything is the realization of what a sinner I am. There are times when I have been ashamed of witnessing to Christ, because doing so would have put me in a tough spot or been embarrassing. But the challenge is always to be able to deny oneself completely – and to give *everything*. We don't know what God is going to ask of us. But if we deny ourselves and take up the cross of Christ, it will not only give us great peace of heart, but also great joy. How much I long to be ready when God calls me home!

My wife and I have been present at many deaths. It is quite obvious when a dying person has used his life in service to others. The peace he has can be seen on his face and felt in the room. But when someone has lived for himself, dying is a palpable struggle, and death an ugly specter. Such people are fearful of what is to come. And even if we have lived a life of service, we may occasionally have reservations; my father told me he often asked himself whether he would be able to say of his life, "It is fulfilled." But we must not doubt that we can find peace in our last hour. Pastor Christoph Friedrich Blumhardt writes:

> Life's most important question is: have I completed my mission on earth? If I have, I can die joyfully. That is why Jesus said, "It is finished." Sorrow lies in our failure to become whole. We weep because we drag along so much that is unfinished. But God will...make right again whatever is broken and set us on a new footing. What we have not been able to finish, he will complete for us, if this is our true longing.

If we live for service, and if we practice forgiveness, we will be ready for God's appointed time. None of us knows the hour of our death; Jesus says it will come like a thief in the night (Matt. 24:43). Not all of us may have the chance to find reconciliation as Ben and his sons did. But all of us, when we are troubled or fearful, can hold on to this promise of Jesus:

> Do not let your hearts be troubled. You believe in God; believe also in me. My Father's house has many

rooms; if that were not so, would I have told you that I am going there to prepare a place for you? And if I go and prepare a place for you, I will come back and take you to be with me that you also may be where I am. You know the way to the place where I am going. (John 14:1–4)

Richard Scott
"I want to use whatever time I have left
to point people to God's kingdom."

9

Saying Goodbye

As we near death, there are always practical matters to attend to, but we should not let these distract us. After all, the close of life is a time to turn our hearts to spiritual and eternal matters.

All the same, it is never amiss, while we still can, to make clear what we wish to happen upon our death. This can be finalized in a will and agreed to by the affected parties. To make the departure easier, it is vital that no room is left for disagreements over inheritances or other financial matters. Did not Jesus say, "You cannot serve both God and money" (Matt. 6:24)? Peace is far more valuable than any bank account.

Although every situation is different, and I would never presume to tell any family what to do, I would caution anyone against trying to prolong life through artificial means. The fact is that this or that medical intervention may keep someone alive but still fail miserably in relieving suffering. It may also prolong the process of dying and burden a body or soul that is seeking release. On top of this, such care is extremely expensive. There is a time for each of us to go, and simply accepting that can bring us, and our loved ones, much peace, most likely more than an additional few weeks of "life" would.

There is widespread agreement with these sentiments within the medical community and among the aged: witness the rise of the hospice movement over the past few decades. Why, then, do so many people still die attached to tubes and in the sterile environs of an ICU rather than in their own bed? In many cases, people are simply uninformed and don't know what their choices really are. Unless older people have made their wishes known, their families will reflexively rush them to the emergency room without thinking through the consequences.

How to find peace over the inevitable death of a friend or family member is never easy, but we can be clear about one thing: we will not find peace ourselves, or bring peace to others, by ordering more tests or authorizing more procedures. Indeed, I have seen situations where an amazing serenity is given in which death can be faced together; for instance, when an informed decision to remove life support is made – one that the family is confident respects the dying person's wishes. In such circumstances, entrusting a loved one into God's hands brings peace.

When and how we actually say goodbye is not important; it's the very act of saying goodbye that counts. I have never forgotten what my brother-in-law Klaus Meier experienced. As the oldest child of the family, he was very close to his father, Hans. When Hans died, Klaus was living in Nigeria, with only limited telephone contact. I would have thought he would find it very hard to be so far away. But before Klaus traveled overseas, he and his father had cleared up any misunderstandings between them, knowing that they might not see each other again. So when Hans died unexpectedly, Klaus managed to let go with an equanimity I've always marveled at. Then again, he knew that he and his father had parted in peace, even though it was months earlier. How different this must be from being consumed by guilt or anger – feelings that burden so many who miss the moment of a parent's death!

I have often heard that at death our whole life, good and bad, is played back in front of our eyes like a film. The past becomes strangely alive as we recall both the good times and the hard times. At such times there may be a tear in one eye and a smile in the other. What is of utmost importance then is that when the last hours come, there is peace in our hearts. We all long that God accepts us into his kingdom.

Most of us will find it hard to accept that the end is coming near. I recall writing to a married couple; the husband was suffering from a terminal illness. I reminded them of the words of Paul: "Therefore we do not lose heart. Though outwardly we are wasting away, yet inwardly we are being renewed day by day. For our light and momentary troubles are achieving for us an eternal glory that far outweighs them all. So we fix our eyes not on what is seen, but on what is unseen, since what is seen is temporary, but what is unseen is eternal" (2 Cor. 4:16–18).

These words express everything. Dying is the final, hardest test of courage. When you know your hours are numbered, it is best to look this straight in the eye and realize that it is only when we lose physical strength that God's love can be glorified. For God's power is not revealed in our strength, but in our weakness (2 Cor. 12:9). At such a time, every moment is precious. Look into the faces of those you love, and laugh and cry. Most of all, pray that the love between you will be strengthened and not weakened.

None of us knows for certain when our time will come, but we can prepare ourselves. When my friend Karl Keiderling, a craftsman, needed major heart surgery, he expected to return home, but he didn't take it for granted. The day before he went into the hospital, he saw to it that all his tools were sharp, "for when I come back." A man of few words, he also got up in church and said that he had no grudges against anybody. He asked for forgiveness if he had hurt anyone. His wife Clare remembers:

> Karl had just read in his Bible that "God sees every sparrow fall," so he put his whole life into God's

hands. I was temporarily wheelchair-bound and worried how we would cope after the surgery when we would both need a full-time caregiver. Karl told me not to worry about a thing. "God has cared for us up till now, and everything will be okay." One thing he especially laid on my heart was, "Now that you can't rush around, you have time for others. Remember to take time to show love."

He told our daughter, "I want to thank you and Mom in advance for standing by me in the hospital. There may be a time when I can't talk to you, but sing to me and talk to me anyway, and I will thank you in my heart." That's what we did, and we are so glad for that, since he never spoke to us again. He died after the surgery.

Like Clare, we must each be prepared to say goodbye to a spouse or friends who might die before we do. This is crucial for our road ahead. God gives us different positions in the battle for his victory. Some of us may be needed as fighters in another world while others will have to stay on this earth a little longer. I've lost countless close friends, fellow pastors, and both my parents. Each time, it hits me a little harder:

it could be me next. But each time, the peace I sense at their passing reminds me of the reward that awaits me, too, if I live out my last days rightly.

In "Terminus," Ralph Waldo Emerson speaks of death as an ocean journey, a picture used by countless other writers as well.

> As the bird trims her to the gale,
> I trim myself to the storm of time,
> I man the rudder, reef the sail,
> Obey the voice at eve obeyed at prime:
> "Lowly faithful, banish fear,
> Right onward drive unharmed;
> The port, well worth the cruise, is near,
> And every wave is charmed."

If we are faithful and can banish fear, we may well experience such a charmed voyage to our next port of call. Even so, saying goodbye to this world may be the hardest thing we ever do. When the time comes, we can find succor in the words of the psalmist, "Cast your cares on the Lord and he will sustain you; he will never let the righteous be shaken" (Psalm 55:22). Sacred music can be especially comforting at such a time. Over the last few years I have come to love the hymn "It Is Well with my Soul." Written by a man who had lost his wife and children, it has tremendous power.

> When peace, like a river, attendeth my way,
> When sorrows like sea billows roll –
> Whatever my lot, Thou hast taught me to say,
> It is well, it is well with my soul.
>
> My sin – O the joy of this glorious thought –
> My sin, not in part, but the whole,
> Is nailed to the cross, and I bear it no more:
> Praise the Lord, praise the Lord, O my soul!
>
> And, Lord, haste the day when my faith shall be sight,
> The clouds be rolled back as a scroll:
> The trump shall resound and the Lord shall descend,
> Even so, it is well with my soul.

How wonderful it is for a person who knows he is going to die soon to be surrounded by people he loves and trusts! Should you, however, find yourself alone at this crucial moment – with no children, spouse, friends or companions around you – take comfort in knowing that Jesus is there with you. He will not forsake you, even if everyone else has. He is waiting to take you into his arms and bring you into God's kingdom. Hold firm to his promises and you will be richly rewarded, especially if your last moments in this world are difficult. Even though you might feel abandoned and alone, put your trust in Jesus, regardless of your circumstances. In Revelation it says:

And I heard a loud voice from the throne saying, "Look! God's dwelling place is now among the people, and he will dwell with them. They will be his people, and God himself will be with them and be their God. He will wipe every tear from their eyes. There will be no more death or mourning or crying or pain, for the old order of things has passed away." (Rev. 21:3–4)

Emmy Arnold

"Each morning when I wake up I am happy
because I have been given another day to love and to serve."

10

Continuing On

THERE IS NO QUESTION that when someone dies, the raw reality of it can be hard for the survivors to bear. They often ask, "Why has this happened to me?" As we think of how our families will cope when we are gone, we can take heart in the words, "The Lord is close to the brokenhearted and saves those who are crushed in spirit" (Psalm 34:18).

Some of the most touching moments I have had as a pastor took place with someone who was losing a spouse after a marriage of forty, fifty, or even sixty years. Most of these couples had a deep faith in God. They had committed themselves to each other for life, one man to one woman, knowing this was the only foundation for a healthy and stable marriage. Their lives were not easy; many of them had endured suffering and hardship. Some survived the Great Depression, while others were veterans of the many wars of the last century. When you've experienced so much together, it's no wonder that the surviving spouse is deeply affected. But in every instance, I noticed a remarkable ability to accept the circumstances.

Thelma, a young woman in my church, noticed this too, with her grandparents, Jim and Jeannette Warren.

> When I finished high school, I had a chance to care for Grandma, who needed full-time care. The way Grandpa cared for her every need impressed me greatly. He slept in a bed right next to Grandma's till the end. Even when the nights were rough, his response was, "I signed up for this sixty-one years ago and I'm not backing down now." When she finally died, Grandpa was at her side. I'll never forget his prayer at her death: "Thank you, God, thank you, thank you for sixty-one years together. Thank you, thank you."

What can give us this sort of peace at the passing of a spouse? I'm not sure I would handle it as gracefully as Jim. Perhaps the key is not to stifle one's pain, but to allow oneself to truly grieve. This is a process which cannot be avoided, yet too often we try to do just that and return as quickly as possible to "normal." Too often we hope that closure is going to come after just a few weeks. But that is not going to happen.

Certainly, life will never be the same for a surviving partner. But through grieving one can find the true peace of Jesus. In many cases, this has to be done alone. Sometimes the most heartfelt anguish happens behind closed doors, without the support of family and close friends. God, however, will always be there.

Without taking time to grieve there will be no proper healing. We must become spiritually quiet and ask God to help us. This need not be a morose thing; it can be redemptive, even joyful. When we discover this, grieving can even honor the deceased.

I experienced this with my parents, Heinrich and Annemarie. My mother was much healthier than my father, but my father outlived her by two years. They had been married for forty-six years. They experienced much from God together and loved one another dearly. The final separation from my mother broke my father's heart. He just did not know how to go on without her. He must have gone through a lot of loneliness, which I as his only son did not appreciate enough at the time.

My father loved these words from Mother Teresa: "We need to find God, and he cannot be found in noise and restlessness. God is the friend of silence. See how nature – trees, flowers, grass – grows in silence; see the stars, the moon and the sun, how they move in silence...We need silence to be able to touch souls."

Those words helped him grieve. After the death of my mother, he spent many hours in silence and prayer, simply in the longing to find God and to be close to him. I should have spent a lot more time with him then, to experience these God-given moments. Too often, I was busy with other things. I have regretted this many times. One thing we did do together after my mother's death was go through the diaries and letters she had written as a young adult, which made her life real to us and drew our family together. This can be a help to any grieving family; to find out if the deceased loved one left behind letters or diaries, and to read them together and relive their life experiences.

Already as a teenager, my father was interested in the medieval mystics, especially Meister Eckhart, whose writings point to the importance of silence and prayer. Throughout my father's life, these two things played an important role, until at the end they became a way of life. Perhaps that is why he was loved by so many people, and why even strangers trusted him and shared their stories with him. Out of prayer and silence, he drew strength to face the temptations and struggles that everybody faces as their life comes to an end, and thus he was able to help others.

Even in their grief, those left behind can be a source of strength and encouragement to others. Gill Barth, a lively grandmother, found out how difficult, yet rewarding, this can be.

The day my husband, Stephan, was diagnosed with an inoperable brain tumor by a specialist, it was hard for me to grasp that his days were numbered – this big, strong man with his love of flowers and gardens, who with his spade had planted thousands of fruiting trees and shrubs. To make matters worse, it happened to be the forty-sixth anniversary of our engagement.

Although our children brought flowers, this hardly made it easier.

But Stephan just said, "I can either just accept this, or I can willingly embrace it and bow down before God." He wiped away the tears running down his cheeks and told me, "Don't be morose! From now on we will celebrate life and have joy with everyone." His total acceptance helped me to drop worry and speculation.

As the days went by, I realized that Stephan was no longer just "my" husband – I had to share him, to open our door to friends and neighbors. Our home was flooded with visitors, bringing memories, laughter, and tears. Every time I thought of the horror of the growing tumor, I had to deliberately turn my thoughts to Stephan's challenge to "celebrate life."

Yet he was not unrealistic, and bit by bit, he let go of things that had mattered to him – the orchards of citrus and grapes he had planted, the key to his favorite truck, his weekly card games with neighbors. Only once did I hear something sad from his lips: "It takes so long to die." Even then it was not spoken as a complaint. After two and a half months the moment of parting came. Through our tears we knew it was a victory and that he had completed his life's task.

Now I was a widow. During the days and months after Stephan died, I was surrounded with love, and this was an enormous help for me, even though I missed him greatly. The first time it rained I ran to get his raincoat – and suddenly remembered that his body lay beneath the earth. Coming home in the evening to find his empty armchair was a continual heartache. So many little things – a song, a memory of a place we had shared, the brilliant stars we used to watch – all tore at my heart and constricted my very breathing.

I tried to hold back my tears so others would not be distressed and only realized later that this was a mistake, that I should have let them flow. I tried to be brave, but I wasn't. I had never known what it meant to lose a loved one. My mother had told me years earlier that after my father died no one ever spoke of him to her, and this made it seem like he never existed. How she longed to hear someone simply say his name! I had not realized my own need for this very basic comfort.

For years I had worked with Stephan in a small company, and now it seemed I had no connection with my coworkers; Stephan had been such a presence in my life and work. It sounds strange, but it was as if I was only a shadow of myself. I tried to find what my role in life should be. I talked with my pastor and began to face the fact that when someone dies, others are left behind to grieve. I met other widows and widowers, who suffered just like me, and found that they were able to come through to a new life by making new connections, new bonds. Just as I had had to "share" Stephan with others as he was dying, so, too, I now had to share of myself, of my time and my energies, and not just grieve for him alone.

It took perhaps two or three years before I was able to do this fully. But I did gain a new peace and a newly thankful heart for the years that Stephan and I had together, and I found that love does not come to an end, but that it reaches from eternity into our hearts here on earth.

My grandmother, Emmy Arnold – Oma, as we called her – is another wonderful example of how grief and separation need not lead to despair and loneliness. She was born to an aristocratic family from Riga, Latvia. Her parents were well-known civic leaders and university professors. In her early twenties she experienced a conversion to Jesus and was baptized. She then married my grandfather, Eberhard Arnold, and in 1920 they started a small intentional community in the German countryside. They put into practice the teachings of Jesus as recorded in the Sermon on the Mount (Matt. 5–7).

Not surprisingly, they were both outspoken critics of Hitler during his rise to power. Then, in 1935, my grandfather died unexpectedly after an amputation to remove an infected broken leg. By 1937, along with my parents and other friends, Oma was forced to flee Germany, eventually sailing for South America through submarine-infested waters at the height of the war.

Oma was a widow for forty-five years. Many times she must have felt very much alone, without the husband whom she so dearly loved. She never, however, felt sorry for herself. She always reached out to other people. Children loved her and flocked to her; she played the piano and loved folksongs and hymns. She was also a good writer and kept up an extensive correspondence with people all over the world.

Oma loved life, especially celebrating Christmas, Easter, and her birthday. She invited many to these celebrations. In her last years, I would often drive her through the beautiful Catskill Mountains, where we'd stop to enjoy a spectacular view or a cup of coffee. The conversations we had about faith, marriage, children, and community influenced me greatly, particularly when she could remember what my grandfather, a noted theologian, felt about a specific topic.

As she became older and weaker, she never stopped reaching out to the many visitors that came to her. When she died at ninety-five, she still radiated joy and enthusiasm. Not just our family, but the many people she had touched over the years, missed her greatly. To me, her legacy reflects the words from Revelation that are inscribed on both her grave and her husband's: "Blessed are the dead who die in the Lord from now on…They will rest from their labor, for their deeds will follow them" (Rev. 14:13).

Not everyone is married, of course, or has a lifelong partner. Not everyone has a relationship as wonderful, and as meaningful to others, as my grandmother did. But every death should be mourned, and every departed soul grieved for.

The peace and purpose we feel in our old age corresponds directly to how well we grieve, and whether we can move from lonely anguish to new joy after a loved one has departed. If we spiral into depression, or dwell too much on past experiences, we may miss the chances offered us to use our grief in a positive way, as my father, my grandmother, and Gill did.

Meanwhile we can rest assured that those who have gone before us to another place are still connected to us here on earth. As my grandfather wrote in his last letter to Oma, "I will pray for you before God into all eternity." Such a thought, even if too great to fully comprehend, will nevertheless be a great comfort to anyone who has faith.

Ellen Keiderling
"These are the best years of my life."

11

Beginning Anew

A DOCTOR WAS ON A HOUSE CALL, and the patient told him that he was afraid to die. He asked what was "on the other side." Hearing a noise outside the door, the doctor responded:

> Do you hear that? It's my dog. I left him downstairs, but he has grown impatient, and has come up and hears my voice. He has no notion what is inside this door, but he knows that I am here. Isn't it the same with you? You don't know what lies beyond the door, but you know that your Master is there.

This story, told by A. M. Hunter, shows the trust with which we ought to approach the end of our lives. Just as we all fear growing old, we also all fear dying. But we will never fully conquer these fears until we realize that we were made not just for this world, but for something greater. If we see death as a stepping stone into another world – as a part of a continuum of the human experience and not as the end of it – we can better deal with it.

As Paul tells us, "Brothers and sisters, we do not want you to be uninformed about those who sleep in death, so that you do not grieve like the rest of mankind, who have no hope. For we believe that Jesus died and rose again, and so we believe that God will bring with Jesus those who have fallen asleep in him" (1 Thess. 4:13–14).

If we truly believe this, we don't need to worry about *what* is on the other side of the door, because we know *who* is there: it is our Master, Jesus. And even as we come to grips with the knowledge that our earthly life could end at any moment, we can live with the certainty that there is a life after death.

I have had a long-running argument with a local restaurant owner who firmly believes that death is the end of everything. He is convinced that there is no life after death, and that there is no heaven. Such a view fails to take into account the greatness of God and his power to redeem and reconcile everything (Col. 1:20).

There are many others who think like this, but the concept of eternity – that is, life after death – is not only a Christian idea. Judaism, Islam, Buddhism and Hinduism all contain a belief in an afterlife. Jesus refers to rooms that are waiting for us in his father's house. George MacDonald elaborated on this when he asked:

> What is it whether we live in this room or another? The same who sent us here, sends for us out of here...I do care to live – tremendously, but I don't mind where. He who made this room so well worth living in, may surely be trusted with the next!

Our lives are brief, like fading flowers. The prophet Isaiah writes that "all people are like grass, and all their faithfulness is like the flowers of the field; the grass withers and the flowers fall" (Isaiah 40:6–7), and the apostle James asks, "What is your life? You are a mist that appears for a little while and then vanishes" (James 4:14). We are foolish if we think we can change this reality. All this would be very depressing, unless we understand that it is part of God's wonderful plan.

As Scripture hints, eternity is not about unending life as we know it; what we know here will soon be over. Eternity is a new life, free of death's destructive powers, a fullness of life where love reigns supreme. The promise of everlasting life has less to do with duration of time and more to do with a certain kind of life – one of peace, fellowship, and abundance – and such a life can begin now.

Deep down we all long for that which God has promised to give: a new kind of existence, a new home with a body that never suffers want or need: "For we know that if the earthly tent we live in is destroyed, we have a building from God, an eternal house in heaven, not built by human hands. Meanwhile we groan, longing to be clothed instead with our heavenly dwelling…" (2 Cor. 5:1–2).

God wants to welcome us all into his kingdom, but we need to begin working toward that here in our earthly lives. What we do in the here and now matters beyond the here and now. We waste so much time in this world with fleeting pleasures, and we forget about the things that really matter. Our life pursuits must not be for food that spoils, but toward that which endures to eternal life (John 6:27).

Such an attitude, or way of life, could be called "living before eternity," where our hearts and minds prepare for the next world, even as we bodily exist in this world. Words attributed to Tecumseh, a Shawnee chief, express this wonderfully:

> Live your life so that the fear of death can never enter your heart...Love your life, perfect your life, beautify all things in your life. Seek to make your life long and its purpose in the service of your people...
>
> Always give a word or a sign of salute when meeting or passing a friend, even a stranger, when in a lonely place. Show respect to all people and grovel to none. When you arise in the morning give thanks for the food and for the joy of living. If you see no reason for giving thanks, the fault lies only in yourself...
>
> When it comes your time to die, be not like those whose hearts are filled with the fear of death, so that when their time comes they weep and pray for a little more time to live their lives over again in a different way. Sing your death song and die like a hero going home.

Living before eternity means not storing up treasures on earth, but storing up treasures in heaven (Matt. 6:19–20). Living before eternity means knowing that we do not live by bread alone but by every word that comes from the mouth of God (Matt. 4:4), and it means knowing that Jesus gives us the living water: "Everyone who drinks this water will be thirsty again, but whoever drinks the water I give them will never thirst. Indeed, the water I give them will become in them a spring of water welling up to eternal life" (John 4:13–14).

As we enter the twilight of our lives, my wife and I have often asked ourselves what is really important. Again and again, we have come to feel that it is to prepare, as best we can, for the moment when God calls us, and to help others when they face death; to stand at their side and help them to cross the bridge from this place to the next.

We would all do well to ask ourselves this question, and it does not matter how old we are. Youth is one of the most wonderful times of life, yet its joys will only be truly complete when young people begin to concern themselves with eternity. The same goes for old age: it can be marked by pain, loneliness, and depression if we don't realize that rather than facing mortality, we are nearing immortality.

To live for eternity, we need faith, the faith that Paul calls "confidence in what we hope for and assurance about what we do not see" (Heb. 11:1). Without faith, we fear the end of our earthly life; with faith this fear is removed. Without faith, we see death as loss and sadness; with faith, death is joyful, even triumphant. Only when we die will new life begin.

In the Gospel of John we are reminded that "unless a kernel of wheat falls to the ground and dies, it remains only a single seed. But if it dies, it produces many seeds" (John 12:24). God wants each one of us to grow and flower and bear fruit in eternity.

As we prepare for eternity, we are faced with the question: What is going to happen to me when I die? But we need not be fearful, because "there is now no condemnation for those who are in Christ Jesus, because through Christ Jesus the law of the Spirit who gives life has set you free from the law of sin and death" (Rom. 8:1–2).

As the ancient Hebrew author of Ecclesiastes so beautifully puts it, there is

A time to be born and a time to die,
A time to plant and a time to uproot,
A time to kill and a time to heal,
A time to tear down and a time to build,
A time to weep and a time to laugh,
A time to mourn and a time to dance,
A time to scatter stones and a time to gather them,
A time to embrace and a time to refrain
    from embracing,
A time to search and a time to give up,
A time to keep and a time to throw away,
A time to tear and a time to mend,
A time to be silent and a time to speak,
A time to love and a time to hate,
A time for war and a time for peace.

The scribe continues:

I have seen the burden God has laid on the human race. He has made everything beautiful in its time. He has also set eternity in the human heart; yet no one can fathom what God has done from beginning to end. (Eccl. 3:2–8, 10–11)

Our lives would be very small indeed if they consisted only of what we experience, touch, and see; but eternity is immeasurable. If we live before eternity, we will see that it is much more real than anything in this visible world. As Paul writes, "Now we see only a reflection as in a mirror; then we shall see face to face. Now I know in part; then I shall know fully, even as I am fully known" (1 Cor. 13:12).

God created each one of us for this world, but he also created us for eternity, and he has something in mind for each one of us. If we live only for this earthly life, it will have its consequences. On the other hand, if we are faithful to God, we are promised that "the righteous will shine like the sun in the kingdom of their Father" (Matt. 13:43). Paul says, "For if you live according to the flesh, you will die; but if by the Spirit you put to death the misdeeds of the body, you will live" (Rom. 8:13). Shouldn't this be our goal?

Of course, as we strive onward, we will make mistakes. But God can use us anyway. Imperfect

Beginning Anew

though we may be in this world, in eternity we can be perfected. The Robert Browning poem that my secretary Ellen loved so much, which I quoted at the start of this book, ends with these words:

> So, take and use Thy work:
> Amend what flaws may lurk,
> What strain o' the stuff, what warpings past the aim!
> My times be in Thy hand!
> Perfect the cup as planned!
> Let age approve of youth,
>   and death complete the same!

Living before eternity gives us an opportunity to conquer death now, even before we physically die. It can help us grasp how God is working in each of our lives, and give us the strength to follow his way in service, love, and forgiveness, so that we can prepare ourselves first for our death and ultimately for eternal life. When God set each of us on our path, he had a purpose for us, a purpose far beyond our imagination. It is through fulfilling this purpose that we will be granted everlasting life.

I am the resurrection and the life. The one who believes in me will live, even though they die; and whoever lives by believing in me will never die. (John 11:25–26)

Postscript

Many have helped my wife, Verena, and me collect the stories in this book. First of all, we want to thank my editor Red Zimmerman and my office staff – Miriam Mathis, Emmy Maria Blough, Else Blough, and Hanna Rimes – who spent countless hours compiling material and reviewing the manuscript. Then there is the entire staff of the Plough Publishing House. Without their help, this book would not be what it is.

Working on this book has given Verena and me a lot to think about. All the fears of old age that are described in this book have also been ours. We can identify with everything that might cross the reader's mind. The answer we have found is to put our trust in Jesus; he will stand by our side when times of testing come. He promised us his peace, "not as the world gives," but the peace "that passes understanding." It is most important to find this peace at the end of our lives. Then we will be able to help others to find it too.

Through interviewing people for this book, Verena and I grew close to dozens of like-minded people of our generation. Each had an incredible story that inspired us to keep going. We discovered that almost every one of them had something in common. They were taught moral values by their parents and teachers in their childhood and youth. They stressed the value of listening to one's conscience regarding right and wrong. Their lives show what a difference it can make when a child grows up in a two-parent home – when husband and wife keep their marriage vows for life, "until death parts you." We hope our generation has not completely failed to pass on this legacy to our children.

On a personal note, it is clear to us that our days in this world are numbered. Rather than being sad about this, we have decided to make it a positive experience. We have received so much love and trust from so many, and approach the future with hope and thankfulness. We have so much to thank God for. He has held us together for over forty-seven years and blessed our marriage with eight children and forty-two grandchildren. Now we have just welcomed our first great-grandchild! When we married, we would have never believed that this day would come.

Thank you for reading *Rich in Years*. We hope you will pass it on and help us spread its hopeful message to as many as possible. We would love to hear what you thought of the book. You can contact us through the publisher at www.plough.com.

The Author

People have come to expect sound advice from Johann Christoph Arnold, an award-winning author with over a million copies of his books in print in more than 20 languages.

A noted speaker and writer on marriage, parenting, and end-of-life issues, Arnold is a senior pastor of the Bruderhof, a movement of Christian communities. With his wife, Verena, he has counseled thousands of individuals and families over the last forty years.

Arnold's message has been shaped by encounters with great peacemakers such as Martin Luther King Jr., Mother Teresa, César Chavez, and John Paul II. Together with paralyzed police officer Steven McDonald, Arnold started the Breaking the Cycle program, working with students at hundreds

of public high schools to promote reconciliation through forgiveness. This work has also brought him to conflict zones from Northern Ireland to Rwanda to the Middle East. Closer to home, he serves as chaplain for the local sheriff's department.

Born in Britain in 1940 to German refugees, Arnold spent his boyhood years in South America, where his parents found asylum during the war; he immigrated to the United States in 1955. He and his wife have eight children, 42 grandchildren, and one great-grandchild. They live in upstate New York.

The Author

Index

Other Titles by the Author

Why Forgive?

No matter the weight of our bitterness, forgiving is the surest way to get out from under it. In this book survivors of crime, betrayal, abuse, bigotry, and war share their amazing stories to challenge and encourage others wherever they are on the road to healing.

Be Not Afraid

In this hope-filled book, ordinary men and women offer hard-won insights on dealing with uncertainty, loss, grief, and the fear of death. Through their real-life stories, Arnold shows how suffering can be given meaning, and despair overcome.

Why Children Matter

Raising a child has never been more challenging. Arnold offers time-tested wisdom and common-sense advice on what children need most, what holds a family together, and how to rediscover the joy of parenting.

Sex, God, and Marriage

A refreshing new look at sex, love, and marriage that sees past the usual issues and gets to the root: our relationship with God, and the defining power of that bond over all other relationships.

Seeking Peace

Where can we find peace of heart and mind – with ourselves, with others, and with God? Arnold draws on the wisdom of some exceptional (and some very ordinary) people who have found peace in surprising places.

Cries from the Heart

An honest look into the lives of men and women who overcame adversity through turning to God – even if their problems worked out in the way they least expected. These stories will reassure those looking for healing and inner peace that even in the deepest anguish, you're never alone.

www.plough.com

What's next?

By now I hope you feel, as I do, that we are on this journey together. No one should have to travel alone. If you haven't already, I encourage you to visit:

www.plough.com

Here you can:

- ◆ Share your thoughts on *Rich in Years*.

- ◆ Get more copies (and my other books).

- ◆ Write to me.

- ◆ Subscribe to the Plough Weekly, a free email newsletter.

- ◆ Sign up for *The Plough*, a quarterly magazine.

Or contact my publisher at:

The Plough Publishing House
151 Bowne Drive, PO BOX 398, Walden NY 12586
T 1-800-521-8011 ◆ 845-572-3455
info@plough.com ◆ www.plough.com

Plough is a not-for-profit publishing house known for quality books on faith, society, and the spiritual life since 1920.